An Orcadian Odyssey

A Memoir

BRYCE WILSON

ORKNEYOLOGY
PRESS

Published by Orkneyology Press
Stromness, Orkney Islands

ISBNs:
978-1-915075-00-0 hard cover
978-1-915075-01-7 paperback
978-1-915075-02-4 ebook

www.orkneyology.com
Book Sales: https://shop.orkneyology.com/collections/orkneyology-press-books

All rights reserved. The contents of this book may not be reproduced
in any form without written permission from the publishers,
except for short extracts for quotation or review.

Typeset by
Main Point Books, Edinburgh

Unless otherwise indicated, text & illustrations
© Bryce Wilson 2022

For Tom and Rhonda

By the same author:

The Lighthouses of Orkney, Stromness Museum, 1975
Sea Haven: Stromness in the Orkney Islands, Orkney Press, 1992
Arthur Dearness & Other Orkney Plays, Herald Publications, 2001
Profit not Loss: The Story of the Baikies of Tankerness, Orkney Heritage, 2003
Stromness: A History, The Orcadian Ltd (Kirkwall Press) 2013
Graemsay: A History, The Orcadian Ltd (Kirkwall Press) 2015
Orkney in a Hundred and One Tales, The Orcadian Ltd (Kirkwall Press) 2018

Books illustrated by the author:

Island Images, Betsy I Skea, The Orkney Press, 1982
The Men of Ness, Eric Linklater, The Orkney Press, 1983
Four Poets for St Magnus, The Breckness Press, 1987
A Haven for Vikings, Orkney Islands Council Museums Service, 1989
Orkney Folklore & Sea Legends, Walter Traill Dennison, The Orkney Press, 1995
The Mermaid Bride and other Orkney Folk Tales, Tom Muir, The Orcadian Ltd, 1998
The Storm Witch and other Westray Stories, Tom Muir, Westray Heritage Centre, 1999

Contents

Acknowledgements   11
Foreword by Tom Muir   13
Introduction   17

1. **In the Beginning**   21
   Bullets ricocheting off the roofs; the Little Lord Mayor; waxed moustache and walking cane; Don't look up!; guillemot eggs on a string; chased by a gorilla.

2. **Swords to Ploughshares**   31
   A house for Stanley Cursiter; hen houses from army huts; snowmen and sledgers; Isaac, thee workshop's gone!; the clatter of escaping pan drops; the Spice Girls.

3. **'Thirty Days hath September ...'**   45
   I tore down the corridor to be First Oot; A – academic and B – practical; a first brush with publishing; When Penguins and Tigers roamed in Stromness.

4. **Graemsay Days**   49
   Open house: the Enchantress stove; oatmeal and beremeal and maturing cheese; flitting and watering, stooking and carting; a night at the Bu.

5. **Rackwick Days**   54
   We erected our tents at Burnmooth by the great red cliffs; many crofts stood empty and ruinous; a Mecca for artists.

6. **A Visual Education**   61
   Drawing from the human form, and painting from plaster casts; a man of seriously left wing views; the Blue Lampie and Ma Cameron's.

7   'Dis yer mither ken ye're workin?'   63
    A crimson dawn and a calm sea; John D and Chairman
    Meow; her propeller spinning in the air; 'a daring
    young man …'

8   'Another bird that flew …'   67
    Howie with his twin whistles; The Warsiest Portions;
    Back to Denmark; BBC Radio Orkney; The Orkney Press Ltd;
    The Orkney International Science Festival.

9   A Diversion   75
    Getting feet over the door; Stromness in Victorian times;
    The Salving of the German Fleet; The Lighthouses of
    Orkney.

10 Oops!   81
    A Museums Service; artefacts of national importance;
    a programme of exhibitions; he revived the art of story-
    telling; a ruckle o' owld stanes!; a feather in the cap.

11 This Town Shone   91
    Hard trodden, this steep path; merchants prospered from
    needle to anchor; The word of a savage is not to be taken
    for it; So long as you make me glamorous.

12 'He came home'   103
    George Simpson McTavish; joined the good ship *Prince
    of Wales*; an occasional young polar bear when roasted;
    beadwork moccasins.

13 Points of View from Across the Atlantic   112
    Cree fiddlers from James Bay; meeting Mary Bichan and
    others; Northwind Dreaming; a peaceful and lovely place;
    We had the floor, man!!!!

14 'Not bad, for a Shapinsay lad' 133
   A dapper Orcadian exile; spotted in Kirkwall by a ballet
   teacher; artists from around the world; a magnificent house;
   vibrant hosting of dinner parties.

15 Margaret Gardiner & the Pier Arts Centre 137
   Paintings and sculptures by major figures of contemporary
   art!; an uphill battle; the artworks made a stately progress
   northward; Cut the painter!

16 Tales to Dine Out On 149
   Do I detect humour?; exit Atwood, gobbling.

17 Four Poets for St Magnus 155
   A vivacious and slightly scary lady; *Four Poets for
   St Magnus*; drink fueled talk and hilarity; the smell of the
   sea was stronger; I will be back!

18 The Past in the Present 163
   A young man with a camera; Sea Haven, Stromness in the
   Orkney Islands; What about a book on beachcombing?;
   'Bryce, try and keep your eyes open'.

19 The Mermaid Bride 170
   Many tales, drams and drawings later; to step into the
   legendary world; I belong tae Glesca!

20 Cath & Karin 173
   Shape-shifting storytellers of Inuit, Maori and Orcadian culture;
   famously performed the Hakka in an international airport;
   we danced hand in hand with the Cree.

21 Babette   177
    Played amid the ruins of Berlin; her wide interests would bring
    her down many paths; A Celebration of Sunrise at the Tomb
    of the Eagles.

22 Back at the Ranch   182
    Stromness Museum was bursting at the seams; this
    generous gesture; the precarious state; Jim Troup and
    Ron Leonard; fanfare and rejoicing.

23 A Pivotal Role   187
    Tankerness House Museum; with a nod to the Baikie
    family; the Orkney Antiquarian Society; opened on
    Friday 31st May, 1968.

24 Retelling the Orkney Story   189
    Stromness, 150 Years a Burgh 1817 – 1967; many
    enlightened comments; John Gunn, an Orcadian who
    lived in Edinburgh; and be read by every Orkney boy and girl.

25 Two Distinguished Historians   194
    William P L Thomson & Ray P Fereday; no history of
    a Scottish county to match it; The Orkney Balfours;
    a rollicking tale.

26 Bursting at the Seams   197
    Plans were approved to double the museum's display
    space; where the Baikies had powdered their wigs;
    Footsteps on the stair!

27 A Tale of Boom and Bust   199
    The all-consuming maw of the supermarkets; the sea has
    once more brought the world to its door; environmental
    expertise around the world.

28 Will Your Anchor Hold?   202
    That ebullient seafarer Robbie Sutherland; recording
    history for the common good.

29 'Cheust sometheen gaan aboot!'   205
    If I got my finger out; Es bueno verte Alfredo!
    Cossacks leapt and sang.

30 Stromness, a History   212
    A flock of straying punctuation marks; 'What on
    earth could you find tae say aboot Graemsay?';
    A gathering of all the Orkney themes.

    In Memoriam   215
    End Piece   218

Acknowledgements

A big 'thank you' to Len Wilson, Gregor Lamb, Gordon Wright, John Gray Snr and Kate Rogers for a critical reading of the first draft; to Babette Barthelmess, Cath Dunsford, Barbara Rae, Tom Muir, Chris Gauld, Duncan Mclean, Doris Stout, Margaret King, Howie Firth and the trustees of the late Elizabeth Graham Scarth, Morag Sinclair and Martin Bernal, for permission to quote from their writings; to Babette Barthelmess, Barbara Rae, Cath Dunsford, Margaret King, Ikuko Tsuchiya, Selena Kuzman, Rebecca Marr and the trustees of the late Sylvia Wishart for permitting the reproduction of their works; to the Orkney Library and Archive and Gray's School of Art Picture Archive; to 'Hutch' for his ready wit, and Sandy Firth for his myriad tales; to Tom and Rhonda for unfailing encouragement and for making this book their first adventure in the Orkneyology Press.

Foreword

'You should be writing all this stuff down,' I said to Bryce as we drank our whisky in a small apartment overlooking the Ljubljana River. The sun was shining and the local coypus were washing lettuce leaves in the flowing water. These were an import to Slovenia that were running wild. So were we. Bryce was in full flow, regaling Rhonda and me with tales of his life story. This was not the first time I'd suggested that he write an autobiography, and it wouldn't be the last time either. This time it just happened in the coolest location and is, therefore, a more suitable setting for an introduction to his memoirs than my being halfway up a stepladder in the Orkney Museum.

I first met Bryce Wilson forty years ago, when still in my teens. I was doing some light volunteering work at what was then the Tankerness House Museum. Little did I know that I would go on to spend most of my working life there and that Bryce would become the most influential man and the dearest friend in my life.

As a dyslexic, I avoided writing like the plague. One day, quite out of the blue, Bryce suggested that I should write new text for our Ba' display. He assured me that I could do it. I was less certain than he was. But I waded into it, and before I knew what was happening I was regularly researching and writing exhibitions.

Next came the books. I had to drag him out of self-imposed retirement as an artist to illustrate a collection of the Sanday folklorist Walter Trail Dennison's folk tales and essays. Bryce had always told me about an aunt who'd been a great baker. One day she'd declared, 'Me baking days is ower!' She put away her baking tins and never touched them again. Like his auntie, Bryce had declared, 'Me drawing days is ower!' But he was eventually coaxed into creating some fabulous images for the Dennison book. This success led to our collaboration on *The Mermaid Bride, and other Orkney folk tales* and then a small collection called *The Storm Witch*, as a fundraiser for the Westray Heritage Centre.

My job at the museum grew under Bryce's guidance, as did our friendship. Without Bryce, I don't know where life would have taken me. But Bryce didn't guide only me; he guided the heritage of Orkney. As Museums Officer, he turned the small Tankerness House Museum into a worthy home for Orkney's archaeology and social history. Its collection is now regarded as one of international importance. Without Bryce, many of the archaeological treasures of Orkney would have taken a one-way journey to Edinburgh. Without Bryce, we would have to travel to the Central Belt to marvel at the Scar Plaque in all its Viking splendour.

Bryce expanded the museum service to include Corrigall and Kirbuster farm museums as well as the Scapa Flow Museum. Not only that, but he redesigned the entire Stromness Museum and was a driving force behind the creation of the Pier Arts Centre. For his services to heritage and the arts, he received a much deserved MBE in the Queen's New Year Honours list, 2014.

In this book, you get a feeling of Bryce's warmth and sense of humour. His stories of Stromness in his childhood are compelling, giving wonderful insight into the everyday life of the town during and after the Second World War. It must not be forgotten that he was an art teacher before he ran away to join the museum.

In Bryce's Odyssey we find stories not only of the great and the good, but of ordinary people. Travels to far-off lands sit beside stories of happy times in Graemsay and Rousay. This book is a treasure trove of tales from the life of one of the most influential Orcadians of the last one hundred years. Bryce brought archaeology, history and art to the general public of these islands through world-class museums and galleries, and also as an historian whose writing brings the past to life in all its humour and tragedy.

Apart from giving a farm boy from Tankerness the opportunity to become a writer, a storyteller and now a publisher as well, I have another important reason to be thankful for Bryce Wilson. Without him *The Mermaid Bride* would never have existed and so I would never have met my wife, Rhonda. She contacted me at the museum after reading that book while researching the historical background of a novel. We had no way of knowing then how important this meeting would become a decade later, when love swept us up in its wings and we were married. We all owe Bryce a great deal. Through his writing, we can get to know him a bit better. Believe me, he is a man worth knowing!

Tom Muir
June, 2022

Introduction

Along with the rest of Britain Orkney emerged after the 2nd World War from a long period of recession and poverty. The creation of the National Health Service and grant-aided Further Education paved the way to a healthier and more egalitarian society. For many, among them poet and painter, musician and entrepreneur, the mantra 'go sooth an' mak' sometheen o' theesel' retreated before a growing appreciation of island life. Many more have come to live in Orkney to escape, as they say, the 'rat race' of urban life. They often enliven island life – socially, culturally and economically.

This is a personal account of the times, an often light-hearted look at the serendipity that has led down unexpected paths. There are tributes to many who have, one way or another, contributed to the life and culture of Orkney and far beyond. Interwoven with the text are drawings and paintings and photographs, glimpses of some of the individual people and places that have contributed to this odyssey.

Bryce Wilson
June, 2022

Are you seated comfortably?
Then I'll begin.

1
In the Beginning

I was born in the early hours of 9th November, 1942. The event was not without drama. My mother suffered a heart attack, and the doctor fainted. My parents, Cathie and Isaac Wilson, had come to live in Stromness from the island of Graemsay, and were among the first tenants of the single-storey council houses in the Sooth End.

Isaac had served apprenticeship at Stanger's Shipyard in Stromness. He had then spent over a decade at sea, sailing as ship's carpenter on cargo vessels to Australia and New Zealand. On one occasion he saved his ship from destruction when the cargo of grain overheated and caught fire. This earned him a substantial bonus.

He passed his seafaring spare time making exquisite ships-in-bottles, often shown at anchor in exotic harbours, including a ship in a giant light bulb for the celebrated novelist Nancy Mitford. He brought home a Japanese tea service with a display cabinet of his own making.

An Orcadian Odyssey

Liverpool Museum commissioned models of an Orkney yole and a Zulu fishing boat. When they were destroyed in the bombing of the museum during the Second World War he made another Zulu – still on display. He turned down the offer of full-time employment.

When Isaac's latest ship *Port Wyndham* was being fitted out on the Thames, Cathie set off to be with him; they lodged for six months with a Docklands family. Conditions were primitive – a dry closet at the bottom of the garden. Theft among '30s stevedores was on an industrial scale. Late at night a van would arrive with rolls of cloth which Cathie cheerfully helped to turn into clothing.

Heading home by train, Cathie reached Thurso in a blizzard. The Aberdeen Airways pilot was reluctant to fly but she insisted and they took off in a white-out: 'We skimmed the top o' the Ward Hill and had a bumpy landing in Stromness.'

The Wilsons lost their first child, then in 1938 on the brink of war my brother William Leonard (Len) was born. Stromness, now army headquarters for Orkney and Shetland, became a 'legitimate' target for Nazi air raids over Scapa Flow. Bullets ricocheted off the roofs of Well Park. Air raid shelters proliferated, and the townsfolk were allocated refuge in the neighbouring farms, should Hitler attempt invasion. Our father's seafaring days were over. Now a member of the Home Guard (with his rifle behind the kitchen door and bullets on the mantelpiece),

In the Beginning

he worked as foreman joiner for the local builder Binnie Harvey, erecting camps for a huge influx of service personnel.

By the time I arrived on the scene, with Churchill in command the Scapa Barrage had scuppered German air raids, and the course of the war was turning against Hitler. Our maternal grandmother favoured marking this turn of events by naming me 'Winston Churchill Wilson'. Unaware of that near miss I spent a remarkable amount of time asleep. Out around the shore with the pram, Mum was joined on her walk by the wife of an army officer, an Indian woman. 'She seemed a bit self conscious and glad of the company.' As time passed, on fine summer days neighbouring doors stood open. For Emily Watt I was 'Little Lord Mayor', having been born on Lord Mayor's Day. My world expanded. We

In the Beginning

picnicked at the Point of Ness. Father rolled up his trousers and said 'I'm off to Graemsay!' 'Daddy, Ah'm coman too!' I tripped and fell face down in a rockpool.

Our mother was forthright and fun loving, kind-hearted and quick-witted: 'I sometimes don't know what I'm going to say until I've said it!' The firstborn of her family she had been the centre of attention. Aged three, she resented the birth of her brother George: 'Pit him in the middeen an' pit a flag[1] on him!' She spent a lot of time with her grandmother 'Ma o' Windywaas', the long-lived matriarch from whom she inherited her lively wit and strength of character, and many tales of Graemsay life.

When she was fourteen years of age, her teacher, Mary Linklater, cousin to the novelist Eric Linklater, pleaded with her father William Ritch to allow her to continue her secondary education in Stromness – but he would have none of it. In the custom of the time she would leave school and assist her mother with the growing family. In her teenage years she experienced a serious bout of rheumatic fever that would affect her in later life. Then an appendectomy brought her to Edinburgh. She recalled how she was met by friends at Leith Docks. Teddy Tait[2] grabbed her suitcase and off they set, capering and laughing all the way up Leith Walk and across Auld Reekie to the Royal Infirmary of Edinburgh. She smiled at her naïvety. 'Which Church do you belong to?' 'The Graemsay Church.' A big black man wheeled her to the operating theatre. 'I thought me last hour had come!' Recuperation meant lying still on her back for three weeks. When she at last got home to Graemsay Andrew o' Ramray said, 'Lass, I thowt wae wid nivver see thee again.' On another occasion the operating theatre lived up to its name. Fully conscious, she saw her tonsils dangling from forceps before serried ranks of students.[3]

Outgoing and good-looking, Mum had been well supplied with suitors, Mary Linklater's brother among them, and the seafaring son of a Graemsay lighthouse keeper. The latter romance came to an end when a letter was snatched and read by a group of mischievous lads – and she was blamed. At length she fell for another seaman – her first cousin, the darkly good-looking Isaac Wilson – and the knot was spliced at Windywalls in Graemsay's last barn wedding. They left the island for a spanking new home with all mod cons – a council house, number 15 Well Park, in the South End of Stromness overlooking the esplanade.

Back in the days of 'meat and two veg' Mum was an adventurous cook. I distinctly remember at barely three years of age sitting at table with 'spoon and pusher', being tempted with a little food of a greenish tinge – my first curry. She was also quick off the mark with Italian fare – spaghetti bolognese and beef lasagne – but never lost her appetite for traditional treats. She would buy a bag of sids (oat husks) from the Birsay mill, ferment them in a bucket of water to make sooan scones, or to be supped raw with sugar – delicious.

In the days when housewives dressed up to go shopping Mum was dubbed the Princess of Well Park; Ruby Brown (George Mackay Brown's sister) was the Duchess. As we walked 'north' to the shops, the first port of call might be to Rachel Smith's in Alfred Street to pay the weekly grocery bill, and for the bairn to receive a sweetie! (Rachel was famous for making 'clagam', a toothsome stick of molten sugar.) I endured seemingly endless adult conversations. We called in turn on a series of seafaring uncles and aunts. At Charlie and Bella's home, 'Sunnyside', formerly part of Login's Inn, a profusely carved Burmese chair graced the hallway, and elephants trumpeted on the mantelpiece.

Charlie Ritch and his brothers Magnus and George Robert began their careers on sailing ships, rounding the Horn 'before the mast'. They moved on to steam. The benign and portly gentlemen that I remember, with waxed moustache and walking cane, had been in their

Brown's Close, looking to Couper's dairy, Alfred Street, 1960s.

prime 'tough to a degree – and capable'. As young men, all three became ship masters. Charlie was obliged to shoot the cook who was rampaging with a cleaver. The 'flamboyant' Magnus, according to a ship-mate, 'was known in every port on the Australian coast.' Reputedly the amateur heavyweight boxing champion of Scotland, he was once ambushed by two men at his cabin door. An officer recalled: 'I heard two loud bangs, saw both unconscious on the deck, and heard Magnus's drawl, "Mr Smith, carry this carrion for'ard ... Mr Smith, I said drag". Entering New York in a blizzard the men objected to being on deck, so he chained the ringleaders to the rails on the forecastle head, and all went well'.[4] When in 1917 his ship was torpedoed near Malta, she was lost with one crew member. Magnus Ritch drunk was better than all the rest sober, it was said, but drink did him no favours when he arrived at a directors' meeting in London worse of the wear, and he ended his career as mate on a humble Stromness coaster.

George Robert thought nothing of quelling disaffected and mutinous crewmen by drawing a gun and firing over their heads. He survived the loss of two ships in the Great War, but rose to be the company's first Marine Superintendent, supervising the construction of their new fleet of motor vessels at Harland and Wolff's yard in Belfast. In his and Aunt Lizzie's fine home, 'Rosslyn', on Franklin Road, a huge shipbuilder's mirror-backed half-model of *King Bleddyn* was affixed to the stairway, and a great stuffed alligator kept watch over the sleeping quarters.

Passing through Alfred Square, Mum cautioned, 'Don't look up!' I did of course, and there was 'Auntie' Polly at her window, beckoning. Polly Wishart had in her youth set off to wed her gold-digging betrothed in the Yukon. With one foot on the gang-plank of *St Ola*, she hesitated: 'Polly, will thoo go, or will thoo no?' Polly went, off on horse-back over the Rockies and married her beloved. Three months later he died in a rock fall.

At Melvin Place lived our father's aunt 'Maddie'. She had left Graemsay to keep house for her widower father James 'Cutty' Wilson, who in his youth had crewed on the Hull whaler *Truelove* in Arctic waters, and later on vessels trading across the Atlantic. He retired in Stromness and occupied his time wildfowling with visiting 'shooters'. It was remembered that in his dotage he still bore a shotgun around the town – when a selkie cavorted by the piers he instinctively shot it, to the dismay of many. When Maddie was at last left on her own she rented out half of the house, and the semi-basement, for a modest income. In the garden she kept a few hens. When she died, among the contents of the house were guillemot eggs on a string, two ship dioramas made by her father and a large piece of whalebone.

A few yards past Melvin Place at the top of a stepped close lived 'Jamesie', the eldest of the Ritch brothers. He had been ship's carpenter, sailing many times around the Horn on the wool clipper *Cromdale*, on at least one occasion felling a tree to replace a broken mast. Jamesie spent his retirement building dinghies and exchanging yarns with old friends in a shed on Gray's Pier.

Tramping past the Stromness Hotel we encountered a

gentleman clad in tweeds and plus fours. Who was that? 'Oh, just a big snob,' said Mum. 'That's what I want tae be when I grow up!'

Memories of the war are scant. I have no recall of wandering onto the esplanade and halting a convoy of army vehicles, but I do remember being issued with a Victory Badge, taking part in the Victory Parade, and being chased by a gorilla.

1 Flagstone
2 Later a well-known Stromness dentist
3 Before the National Health Service surgery was free if performed before students – hence 'operating theatre'
4 *Idyll of the Kings: The History of the King Line 1889–1979*, Alan S Mallet, World Ship Society, 1980

2
Swords to Ploughshares

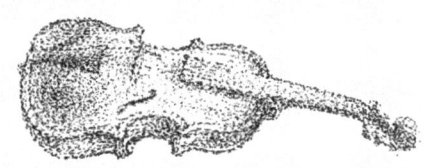

With the onset of peace my world changed. Gone were the friendly neighbours. We had come to live in a tall, cold and draughty house misnamed 'Sunnybrae', on the Back Road ('Snob Hill'), surrounded by the deserted huts of the Royal Corps of Signals – across the road in Quildingsquoy stood their carrier pigeon sheds. An elderly rat lived in the coal shed, and mice went about their business through holes in the skirting boards. Sunnybrae had been built as a retirement home by the cattle dealer John Matheson from the farm of Cauldhame in Stromness parish. Our grandfather William Ritch, who had not accepted the dealer's offer of a partnership, turned his spyglass on Stromness and remarked: 'There's Matheson's hoose going up.' Sunnybrae stood roofless throughout the Great War. John Matheson died soon after moving in. His large family spread around the globe while his daughter Annie, a teacher, lived out her life at Sunnybrae.

One of our father's postwar jobs for Binnie Harvey had been to convert Stanger's Shipyard, where he had served apprenticeship, to a house and studio for the artist Stanley Cursiter. He described how Cursiter had provided the tar-bespattered weather boarding from old shipyard sheds to line the stairwell. Once, as a child, when the Cursiters were absent I peered through a back window – and from time to time returned, for there, glowing in the shadows, was one of his finest paintings, *House of Cards*.[1] Years later, when I had returned from study at Gray's School of Art to the post of itinerant art teacher in Orkney, I was commissioned to arrange an exhibition of paintings for Stromness Shopping Week. I had the temerity to approach Stanley Cursiter, now living in retirement with his wife Phyllis on a pier off Victoria Street in the house he had converted from the stables of the former Masons Arms Hotel. Cursiter kindly loaned several works, including the medallions from which Reynold Eunson made carvings for the St Rognvald Chapel of St Magnus Cathedral. The Cursiters would be away from Orkney during and after Shopping Week. Would I look after the paintings until their return? Throughout that summer, Cursiter's Futurist painting *The Sensation of Crossing the Street – West End, Edinburgh* hung in our living room.

During this visit with Stanley Cursiter I incurred his impatience by announcing that I was going over to Hoy to paint in the valley of Rackwick, then a growing source of inspiration for painters and poets. Why did I not stay at home and paint Stromness?

A decade would pass before I again encountered Stanley. Having arranged a summer exhibition, *The Lighthouses of Orkney*, in Stromness Museum, I was a guest of the Lighthouse Commissioners during their annual cruise on board NLS *Pharos*. Among other guests was Stanley Cursiter, now a widower. He greeted me warmly and complimented me on the history of the Orkney lighthouses that I had written for the exhibition booklet. So the following Saturday morning I found myself seated at his harbour window, with pen in hand to sign his copy while he dispensed sherry and passed scraps of food through the open window to Sigurd, the hirpling seagull.

Swords to Ploughshares

Of the redundant army Signals huts in Sunnybrae's park, the officers' mess became a retirement home for our maternal grandparents from Graemsay. Sunnybrae was made mouse-free and comfortable; flowers and vegetables took over from nettles and thistles. A Raeburn stove now provided for hot water, cooking and baking. Such was Mum's joy at this development that behind the plumber's back she blew him a kiss. When Dad returned from work my first words were, 'Daddy, Mum kissed the plumber!'

By this time our father had new employment. He was now Burgh Surveyor, appointed by the Town Council of Stromness on a weekly wage of £7 with a handful of labourers to run the public services – water supply, sewerage, street sweeping and maintenance – and clerk of works for council housing schemes. At home there was also much activity. Despite being ordered off the park by a territorial toddler, workmen used hut timber to build 'Grunavoe' for 'Baffin Bay' (former Hudson's Bay Company man Jimmy Sinclair) and his wife Helen. A Nissen hut became a chicken hatchery, and other huts provided timber for hen houses. In the evenings we turned eggs in heated incubators, and before school Len and I each had a pig to clean out and feed, keeping the profits!

Chief Engineer John Vass of NLB *Pole Star* lived with his family at Maya Cottage, shoulder to shoulder with Sunnybrae across the old Ootertoon road. When they moved away, leaving us a treasure of glass marbles, Maya Cottage became home to Eoin and Audrey Mackay, and Audrey's parents the Inneses. Mrs Innes would come over for a cup of tea. When on the death of her husband Mum offered her condolences, she replied, 'My dear, I grieved for him long ago.'

A spirited entrepreneur, Eoin's father built Mackay's Stromness Hotel. From the Glasgow International Exhibition of 1888 he had reputedly imported and re-erected the Swedish exhibit as the Standing Stones Hotel, and purchased the Kirkwall Hotel; but Eoin's life had more style than substance. Cars were not numerous in Stromness in the '50s, but the Mackays had one, as Audrey would say, 'in the garaage'; and a racing dinghy in the harbour. Eoin invested in Rendall's printing shop in Victoria Street, and Mortimer's butcher shop in Graham Place, but he was, shall we say, not a morning person. At last the Mackays moved south, where Audrey took the reins and successfully ran the Tweeddale Arms in Gifford, Midlothian.

An overnight hurricane in 1952 brought Mum from bed to window: 'Isaac, thee workshop's gone!' Len remembers:

> To leeward of the Nissen huts was a wooden hut which had been the Officers' Mess. It had been converted into a dwelling house for our grandparents. They called it 'Learig', for they'd lived in 'Windywalls' all their married lives. It still stands there today. Anyway, Dad was frightened that it would get damaged by the corrugated iron sheets from his workshop, for 'Learig' was still just a wooden hut with a sheet iron roof. If a window got broken the roof would go off. He went out through our front door, for it was on the lee side of the house, and he had to crawl the 300 yards to 'Learig'. It was okay and he crawled back again. This was a dangerous operation for there was so much debris flying about... Our neighbour, Andrew Wards' hen houses had come over the dyke and lay broken in our field, his hens literally 'gone with the wind'. Luckily our own hen houses remained intact. This was the heyday of the famous Orkney egg and there were thousands of hens in the county. Many perished when their houses were smashed or they were swept out to sea.

In the morning we looked out and admired the wallpaper of the now roofless huts of the Attery (Auxiliary Territorial Service – women's branch of the army), still in use as 'temporary' council housing. No-one had been injured. Families got shelter in the redundant St Peter's Manse. Sheila Lobaczewski summed up:

> *Better than the Attery, living in a tent!*
> *Better than the Attery, pay no rent!*

An Orcadian Odyssey

Len continues:

> There were many stories circulating after the storm, some fantastic, some funny, like the woman who went out at her door and lost her nightdress, and some definitely tall. One wag in Stromness was heard telling seriously how he opened his door and the ceiling hatch went straight up into the loft, 'an the wife's fur coat disappeared right efter it!'

A field away to the west, in Seaview lived the retired farmer Andrew Wards with his wife, their daughter Muriel Nicholl and her children Colin and Anna. A century before, our great-grand-aunt Mary Ritch had lived there with her husband Captain Magnus Lyon of the *Royal Mail*, first steam-powered mail service on the Pentland Firth. Beyond Seaview was the dairy farm of Broonstoon, home to the Learmonth family from Sanday. The Learmonths and the Nicholls, and 'Dusty' Clouston's boys in Springfield Crescent, were our playmates.

The view from Sunnybrae took in a broad sweep from the Harray hills across Stenness and Orphir, South Ronaldsay, Flotta, Cava and Graemsay to the hills of Hoy. It was broken only by the huge St Peter's Manse. The Manse Park had shared with Sunnybrae the Royal Signals camp; it was now the perfect adventure playground, with tumbled foundations and barbed wire and rusty iron among nettles and dockans and thistles. A big boy, Freddy Young, held court in an Anderson shelter. When the Reverend Mair Hutcheon died and the family were packing up, his daughter opened wide the kitchen window and dished out toys from another era. Warm summers gave way to cold winters, sufficiently so for cinder-eyed pipe-smoking snowmen to watch snowball fights at every corner; cloggers, and sledgers on the 'belly gutser', hurtling from the brae of Oglaby all the way down Hellihole or Springfield Crescent to the street.

The Wilsons were fiddlers, mostly at Graemsay barn dances but sometimes on Arctic whalers. I broke with

tradition and took piano lessons with Mrs Porter. The tall house of Farafield where she lived looked down on the roofless remains of the Old Orkney whisky distillery, which her father had owned. Amid the faded elegance of the drawing room I remember a magnificent dark blue and white Wedgwood dinner service.

While being hopeless at reading music I became adept at playing by ear, handy in later years for late-night parties! In the '50s the Chapple family traded Inverness for Stromness when 'Farquh' (Farquhar), a baker, secured a job at Stockan's. Many who remembered the fun and frolics of army clubs and bars in wartime Stromness were ready for a good time. Betty and Farquh were full of music. They would pack the house with neighbours, sometimes around twenty folk, for a Burns Supper. At New Year their tiny sitting room expanded like Dr Who's Tardis for a steady stream of first-footers – standing room only. I hammered on the piano with Farquh singing and Betty on the accordion. Pamela and Maureen handed out endless jugs of home brew and plates piled high with sandwiches, well into the night.

Among contemporary Graemsay musicians our cousin Ruby (Skinner) Manson was a fine fiddler. Moving to Stromness she joined the West Mainland Strathspey and Reel Society, and played around the parishes with 'Tom on the box'. She joined up with Margaret Leask and Netta Ashburn. The fiddle and accordion trio, affectionately known as 'the Spice Girls', drew crowds to the front bar of the Royal, especially when joined by passengers of MV *St Sunniva* which regularly tied up in Stromness on her way from Lerwick to Aberdeen.

In addition to fiddling, Ruby quietly experimented with painting, dropping coloured ink on paper to see where it led her – finally to a sell-out exhibition at the Bu Gallery in Victoria Street. When she died her many friends gathered in the Town Hall for music and memories, and each was invited to select a teapot from Ruby's extensive collection. Her neighbour Chris Gauld wrote this poem:

Hame

Here's a remembrance,
that'll bring a warm tear to the coldest o' souls.
She wis the best o' Neeb'rs,
would help in a blink.
Mean fiddler, but no mean o' pocket.
And I mind on her saying to me,
'I always think it's like getting a present,
when someone gives you money back'.

Well she's away to wherever we go,
maybe somewhere over that rainbow,
who knows?
The Shelties[2]
that have shifted in noo,
short o' furniture so I kent whit to do.
Offered them an auld unit she'd gifted me,
they took it,
gladly.
And noo it's hame again.

For Ruby, wherever she is.

Ruby would have laughed, as she always did.

The hard physical work of house-keeping and poultry farming took its toll on Mum. Having suffered a severe bout of rheumatic fever in her teens, not to mention a mild heart attack on my birth, in her forties heart damage became apparent. The poultry farming came to an end, and domestic activities were much curtailed. We acquired the town's first electric washing machine. Norman Mowat 'the Hydro man' said he wouldn't need to advertise them: 'Everybody'll hae wan noo.' The park was turned over to the grazing of sheep and cattle and on one occasion, when Tom Learmonth sowed a crop of oats, a corncrake disturbed our sleep.

We had extended our smallholding by renting Quildon's park next to ours. When Mrs Young said, 'It's of no use to us any more – would you like to buy it?' Father explained that it was no longer of use to us either, so turned down a generous offer. A decade or so later the council acquired it for housing – Grieveship West. Father had by this time retired, but accepted the job of Clerk of Works, from a little shed provided in our back garden. Across the burn, the site of Grieveship East needed explosives to shift the granite of Brinkie's Brae. Sunnybrae shook to the blasting, and one sizeable chunk of granite sailed over the house to land among the cabbages. As the years have passed, all of the ceilings of the house have had to be replaced.

'Our eyes met.'

Father enjoyed his work as Burgh Surveyor, and only retired when he had grown too deaf to follow business at council meetings. He told us that once when his ship was docked in New Zealand he discovered that an immigrant from Stromness had come aboard and was helping himself in the paint store. He got off with a reprimand. Many

An Orcadian Odyssey

Isaac Wilson

years later it was announced at a town council meeting that they were about to have a visit from a Stromness man who had risen to a prominent position in local government in New Zealand. In he came. 'Our eyes met,' said Father.

The town council in their wisdom had decided to replace the street flagstones with concrete slabs which their labourers would make. Father recommended a minor rise in pay as they were now working as tradesmen. When the council threw out this proposal he said, 'That's all right then. Slab-making will cease forthwith.'

On retirement Father said, 'It's downhill all the way now.' But he had many fruitful years ahead. He restored a cottage in Puffer's Close, was a founding member of the West Mainland Strathspey and Reel Society, launched a fleet of ships-in-bottles and crafted scores of wedding cogs. Time took its toll. The hedges and trees that he had planted and tended arose in wild profusion, beloved of birds and mice and patrolling cats.

Back in the '40s and '50s most folk still attended the Kirk, and they had plenty of choice. Even though the splits of the 19th century had been mended, there were still three Church of Scotland congregations in Stromness and three ministers, tripping over one another. (Some folk who loved singing went to them all!) We attended St Peter's, the parish kirk that had been constructed in 1817 on the site of an earlier one at the head of the Kirk Road, with a huge gallery, to accommodate no less than 1200 souls. Two magnificent stained-glass windows relieved the gloom, while Stewart Wilson (no relation) pumped the bellows to extract a wheeze from the ancient and asthmatic pipe organ. In a centuries-old ritual the beadle Willie Leslie solemnly ascended the pulpit stair bearing Bible and Prayer Book, followed by Mair Hutcheon, the frock-coated minister. Seemingly endless sermons were punctuated by the clatter of escaping Pan Drops and outbreaks of barely suppressed mirth. After Mair Hutcheon's death the congregation moved in beside that of the former United Presbyterian kirk in Victoria Street. They bore with them the great stained glass windows and the granite font, but left behind the rare and valuable organ, to be trashed during conversion from Kirk to Youth Centre.

The redundant St Peter's Manse became the 'Eventide Home' (St Peter's House). Among the first residents were relatively fit single people who had lived in farm or domestic service and had nowhere else to turn; colourful

An Orcadian Odyssey

characters among them. Known to her family as 'Auntie Kit', Catherine Thomson from Hoy gave us a 'Kit's eye' view of the state of affairs in St Peter's House, and left the distinct impression that she ran the kitchen. Ned from Deerness went daily down to Rae's Newsagent to collect 'the pippers'. He had an artificial leg which he proudly showed off, covered in pencilled hair. In later years Harry Berry, renaissance man o' Hoy, turned his artistry to decorative nameplates for the residents' doors. And Robert Rendall from Kirkwall, draper, poet, theologian, conchologist, archaeologist and painter, would take his stick and wander up the brae of Quildon to enjoy Scrabble with the Couper sisters, whose aunt had been his kindly host and dear friend in the P'lace of Birsay.

Andrew Kirkness was the first gardener and handyman of St Peter's House. It fell to him to create extensive lawns, shrubberies and flower-beds. In the kitchen garden he built a greenhouse. A friendly rivalry brought him one day to assess the state of Mum's tomatoes. To his dismay he found that one was already ripe, but on closer inspection discovered that it was tied to the plant. 'Ye bitch!' When Howie Firth started a little garden at the head of Springfield Crescent it was secretly laced with poppy seeds. He's still wondering. Ditto the Reverend Hume, were he still with us, who after a kirk jumble sale found an edition of Spurgeon's *Sermons* in his basket.

Those were the times of serious spring cleaning, when on a sunshine day sheets and blankets were spread in the garden to air. Once, Mum noticed the approach of a not very tall figure. Throwing a white sheet over her head she hid behind the garden dyke, then arose waving her arms, groaning and moaning piteously as ghosts do. Only it wasn't me walking up the path but our lawyer Jackie Robertson. (Should have gone to Specsavers.)

She once revealed that she would have loved to have studied Medicine. She enjoyed the many aspects of community and domestic life: the Scottish Women's Rural Institute,[3] the Flower Club, the Church Guild, and was a founder member of the Ladies' Debating Society. (The Stromness Debating Society, an exclusively male preserve, deigned to invite the ladies to their annual dinner. 'Will you have a drink, Mrs Wilson?' 'Yes, I'll have a double whisky!' It never arrived.) She practised gardening, cooking and baking, knitting and crocheting and dress-making with great skill. She baked sooan scones on the SWRI stand of the Highland Show. One of the team remarked, 'I always thought your mother was very straight-laced till I heard her tell a story.' (She didn't repeat the story!)

When blankets went out of fashion Mum travelled the isles and parishes showing how to turn down-filled quilts into duvets. In Shetland to judge handicrafts, she was astonished to find that she might award several First and Second and Third Prize tickets to competitors in the same field, a generosity of spirit quite unheard-of in Orkney! Well into her eighties, she was matriarch to an extended and far-flung family. When she died there were many tributes, among them: 'She was one of the few people who really cared about others'; 'I never knew anyone who got so much fun out of life'; 'I miss meeting yer Mum on the street, she always had something weeked tae say!'; 'It was a privilege to know her'; 'A lovely lady'. Amid all she was a great storyteller, imbuing us with tales of Graemsay life.

1 Now hanging in the Baikie Drawing Room, Tankerness House
2 Shetlanders
3 Now the Scottish Women's Institute

3

'Thirty Days hath September...'

At not quite five years of age, I was sent to school (my satchel a First Aid bag found among the army huts). In the Infant Class, presided over by the benign Miss Smith, the walls were adorned with cards showing numbers in domino layout – still imprinted in my mind. Learning by rote and speaking 'proper' were accompanied by the screech of slate pencils and the inexorably slow advance of the hands of the clock. This little ditty was memorised:

> *Thirty days hath September,*
> *April, June and November:*
> *All the rest have thirty-one*
> *Except for February alone,*
> *Which hath twenty-eight days clear,*
> *And twenty-nine on each Leap Year.*

While still in the Infant Class, one morning when we were leaving the classroom, thinking that it was dinner time I tore down the corridor to be First Oot, and ran all the way home. 'You're home early the day.' Back at school after dinner nothing was said, but then Mr Groundwater the headmaster came in and stood before me with Miss Smith and said from a great height: 'You'll not do that again, will you, Bryce?' Not, however, explaining of what I was guilty. (But I discovered that I had skipped PE – full marks!)

The years passed. By the time I reached the Secondary Department, Len had left school at sixteen for a seafaring career. A ship master uncle advised that he gain a qualification that could be of use 'when he had had enough of the sea', so he attended Leith Nautical College to become a radio officer. After four years at sea he had apparently 'had enough'. His radio qualification came in useful and he spent most of his working career with the Civil Aviation Authority, finally in care of navigation aids at Kirkwall and Wick Airports.

In the Higher Grade we were streamed by examination into 'A' (academic) and 'B' (practical). Since dyslexia had not yet been discovered, highly intelligent children could be regarded as 'no hopers' and relegated to the 'B'

Stromness Academy Class 2A, 1956
Back L–R: Isabel Muir, Freda Merriman, Evelyn Couper, Raye Lennie, Connie Wishart, Moira Sinclair, Aileen Fiddler, Fielda Flett, Minnie Leask, Kathleen Grieve.
Middle L–R: Brenda Stockan, Sheena Sinclair, Hazel Garson, Mary Learmonth, Marian Petrie, Betsy Bottomly, Isobell Bolt, Hilary Gibson.
Front L–R: Alan Twatt, George Berstan, Bryce Wilson, Edna Spence, Iris Brass, Inga Brown, Isabel Work, Jean Macdonald, Robert Mackay, Gath Cumming, Rankine Firth.

grade. My cousin Gordon White beat the system. He left Stromness for London, became a full-time union official and ended his career as Union Leader for Airline Cabin Crew throughout Britain. For me, a first brush with publishing came in the form of *The Sunnybrae Special*, occasionally produced on the school's 'Banda' copier, and involvement with the annual school magazine, printed at Rendall's in Victoria Street.

Senior pupils signed up for a school trip. In the care of four or five good-time teachers we set off by the Ola, bus, ferry and train all the way to Paris. What was a bidet – somethen tae wash yer feet in? What's on the menu? Boeuf sous-cuisinière avec légume al dente! We said hello to the *Mona Lisa*, posed in the Hall of Mirrors, paid our respects at the Tomb of the Unknown Soldier, endured the dizzy heights of the Eiffel Tower, and sussed out the wine bars while the teachers sampled Le Moulin Rouge.

Fifty years on, Morag Sinclair remembered:

> *When Penguins and Tigers roamed in Stromness*
> *And a Queenie was no' jist a clam*
> *These are the days that helped make me*
> *Into the 'me' that I am.*
> *When a Sniff wasn't a sign of a cold*
> *And a Moonie a weird holy guy*
> *And a Skene was much more than just only a flock*
> *O' migrating geese in the sky.*
>
> *When MacInnes did more than paint cliffs and*
>   *rough seas*
> *And Pi-a was not always square*
> *And Myrtle was more than a bonnie wee bush*
> *She made the most wonderful fare!*
>
> *When Sinclair made us all do physical jerks*
> *And Annal made us dance with the boys*

*And Rosie meant not only young healthy cheeks
But a bounce and melodious noise.*

*When Gobbie wisna just a big sweetie
And Frenchie was more than a condom
And a Bunny did more than just hop and eat grass
And live in a comfy wee hutch-home.*

*When an Onion did more than jist flavour your mince
And Mackie made more than ice cream
And Clootie did more than jist wipe up your spills
These are the days of my dream.*

4

Graemsay Days

In my teens in the '50s I spent holidays with Uncle James and Auntie Cathy on the 80-acre croft of Garson in Graemsay. Childless, they held 'open house' for nieces and nephews from outwith the island, and the children from the surrounding crofts. The flag-roofed dwelling was the greater part of a long, single-storey range, ending with byres and stable. The kitchen, where the stone floor was hidden by stout brown linoleum from a demolished army camp, was heated by the large Enchantress stove that also provided for hot water, cooking and baking. Girnels, for the storage of oatmeal and beremeal and maturing cheese, lined the wall. Above them hung a large mid-19th century

Garson, Graemsay © Ian MacInnes

An Orcadian Odyssey

The Victoress Stove

print of Castle Street, Aberdeen, while the dresser hosted a pair of Staffordshire figurines of General Buller and Lord Roberts on horseback. Each of the three bedrooms opened into the next; one of them had window-glass engraved with a shipping company emblem. Across the close the corrugated iron 'shop', formerly the grocery run by James's mother and sisters, contained a dry toilet, and was furnished with a folding ship's wash stand removed from the blockship *Inverlane* in Burra Sound. In the wooden porch sheltering the door of the house from winter and summer gales stood the water buckets, filled from a well at some distance down the brae, at Quoys Noust on the Bay of Sandside – summer anchorage of the yole *Jane*. House and steading were now lit by an oil-powered 'startomatic' electricity generator which came to life with the first flick of a domestic light switch, and stopped with the last switch-off at night.

In the sheds were the ploughs and the tractors: a wee grey 'Fergie' and two Fordsons (the 'spade lug' was funded through lobster fishing). There was a self-binder for harvesting, a rake for the hay and the 'milk hoose' for making butter and cheese. Flitting and watering and milking the kye, feeding the hens, collecting and washing the eggs, turning the cream separator and the butter kirn, coleing and carting the hay and building the stacks, stooking and carting the sheaves and building the screws, were all activities in which the youngsters were expected to assist. From time to time we were treated to a fishing trip, experiencing the thrill of a hard tugging on the line and the landing of haddock or lythe or a supper of cuithes.

'He's no' an ill sowl ...'

It was a beautiful summer evening. A thundery plump had halted the harvest, and the still air was heaving with midgies. 'It's too fine a night tae bide in. The mudgiks areno' fond o' the sea. Wae'll tak a luk ower tae Hoy, an' pay Jock Spence a visit,' said Uncle James. So off we set past Hoy Low Lighthouse to Burra Sound, negotiated the blockships, dropped anchor in the Bay of Creekland and pulled ashore in the flattie.

Fending off battalions of Hoy midges, we strode past the kirkyard on the road to the Bu. Jock Spence reputedly made two brews of ale – a mild one for welcome visitors, and a very strong one for others. (One caller apparently fell

An Orcadian Odyssey

Uncle James

over on the way home and spent the night in the ditch.) But he had an extraordinary affinity with animals. It was to him that folk went for help and advice when a farm animal was ailing. 'He's no an ill sowl,' said James, who could himself charm selkies from the sea without really trying. Soon the ancient mansion of the Bu came into sight, gable to the sea and surrounded by trees. Jock Spence met us at the gate and brought us indoors. The low-beamed kitchen had a blue stone floor and a great dresser and plate rack, worn and blackened with age. Soon, Jock produced a jug of ale, poured James a glass and started to pour another. I must have looked apprehensive. 'Aer thoo faered fur me?' asked Jock, giving me a sidelong glance and pouring a brimming glass. After a while discussing the crops and the kye Mrs Spence appeared and prepared a supper of bannock and cheese and cake, washed down by a strong brew of tea. On the way back to the boat, I didn't fall in the ditch. (When Dr Johnstone paid his regular visit to Graemsay he reserved Garson as last port of call, there to enjoy a glass of Uncle James's delectable ale.)

'Gather ye rosebuds ...'

James and Cathy spent a long and well-earned retirement in Stromness, with a noust for *Jane*. James continued to go fishing, and the fishermen around the piers claimed him as their favourite 'uncle'. The Kirk had withdrawn Graemsay's lay missionary, and the Manse stood empty. There I spent many idle days, boiling gulls' eggs, reading endless novels, feeding the hungry stove, trimming the smokey lamps, lifting 'cool clear water' from 'the best waell in Gremsa' and combing the shores for driftwood. A sadly deflated plastic woman was washed ashore at Gangsti. (There were at that time hundreds of men on Flotta engaged in building the oil terminal.) Stuffed with hay she was tied to a pier bollard where, like the sirens of old, she lured passing fishermen...

The Oil Lamp

5
Rackwick Days

From the age of eleven I was a member of the Boys' Brigade, formed to instil respect for authority and some basic skills in a motley crew heading for adulthood. I had chosen to avoid summer camp until the brigade captain, Sandy Tait, announced that anyone wishing to qualify for a proposed trip to Golspie the following year would have to take part in a camp in Orkney – in Hoy in the valley of Rackwick.

We erected our tents at Burnmooth by the great red cliffs, a mile of silver sand and massive boulders, hewn and tumbled smooth by Atlantic breakers. Rackwick folk were renowned fishermen, but few of the little crofts were still occupied. The tragic drowning in the burn of two young brothers had led that family to leave the valley, and in a changing world many crofts stood empty and ruinous.

Our BB camp leaders, Sandy Tait and his wife Kitty, went on to rent the croft house of the Moss for family holidays. 'Doc' Johnstone acquired the Mucklehoose, and the Boys' Brigade took a lease on Groups. Rackwick had long

Sandy Tait

Northoose, Rackwick © Sylvia Wishart

been a Mecca for artists, Stanley Cursiter among them. Ian MacInnes now acquired the Noust by the shore (formerly the Test House for the telegraph cable from Caithness), and Sylvia Wishart the Northoose on the brae. The poet and author George Mackay Brown visited and was enthralled; in his wake came the composer Peter Maxwell Davies.

I did not get to know Sylvia until, back in student days, Erlend Brown arranged for himself, Howie Firth and me to stay for a week at the Northoose. Sylvia joined us at the weekend, and others arrived for a convivial evening. This was the start of an enduring friendship. Sylvia was still teaching in Kirkwall, but soon an Arts Council grant allowed her to paint full-time.

The Mowats had not long left the Northoose, and Sylvia lovingly preserved it. On a hot August day friends and relatives joined her in cutting rashes (rushes) while Andrew Kirkness thatched the flagged roof. Sylvia often loaned the Northoose to friends, but spent much time

An Orcadian Odyssey

Brinigar, Innertoon, Stromness

there on her own, painting. One winter she lent a hand to the last crofter, Jack Rendall. A heavy fall of snow engulfed the valley.

Among those who enjoyed the hospitality of Northoose were Chris Bonington, Tom Patey and Rusty Baillie, on their way to being the first to scale the Old Man o' Hoy in 1966. (Sir Chris did it again forty-eight years later to celebrate his eightieth birthday.)

Sandy and Kitty Tait's art graduate daughter Kate, heading home by train, was joined in the refreshment car by a group on their way to 'Oaknay'. Being of a sociable nature she introduced herself as an Orcadian, but she was soon sidelined as the group began to sing the praises of Orkney's bard, George Mackay Brown. When they discussed an intended pilgrimage to Rackwick, fortified by a couple of G&Ts Kate piped up: 'Excuse me, but I was once at a supper table in Rackwick when the painter Sylvia Wishart was moved to hurl the sauce bottle at George Mackay Brown!' Suddenly, all eyes were on Kate.

George in the '60s still frequented the pubs, but he lamented the passing of the 'characters' of whom he wrote, 'Drink unlocked their tongues and made poets of them.' He dedicated his novel *Magnus* to a fellow toper, Attie Campbell. 'The wife's gone – gone forever,' Attie

Rackwick Days

Snow, Rackwick © Sylvia Wishart, 1970

would say, sipping his pint with an air of contentment. On one occasion a health inspector said, 'Your room has a very low ceiling, Mr Campbell.' 'It's a very low man that lives in it,' said Attie. Among other frequenters of the Royal was 'owld Newt', who daily motored from his farm, Newton Hill, and drove back again. One night he went home and died in his sleep, unaware that his raffle ticket had won a cask of ale.

In 1966, BBC Television broadcasted a film based on George's poetry. In response to my letter he wrote: 'I'm really glad you liked the TV poem on Orkney. It seems to have been quite a success, thank goodness, after the alcoholic time there was over the making of the film.' This was the first that most British citizens knew of Orkney, never mind George Mackay Brown. His reputation grew and over the years it brought many to his door. One evening in 1991 a young man caught up with me on the street. He explained that he had just alighted from the ferry, and asked the way to George's house. This was Surinder Punjia, who stayed on in Stromness as a friend and supporter to George during his last years.

An Orcadian Odyssey

Northoose kitchen

'There's a library up the road!'

One of those lured to Stromness by George Mackay Brown was Charlie Senior, from among the poets and painters and writers who swarmed like bees around Edinburgh's Rose Street pubs. A Glaswegian by birth, Charlie took Orkney to heart and came with his wife Carol in the late '60s to live over the brae of Clouster at Quoybow. He published two fine volumes of verse before becoming a purveyor of books and prints, old and new. 'An' hoo long will that lest?' was the street corner refrain: fifty years and counting.

Rackwick Days

Sylvia Wishart (second right) with friends at 'Heatherybraes', Stromness, in the '80s. Foreground, George Mackay Brown

Some customers of the bookshop tried Charlie's patience. One overlong browser earned the rebuke: 'There's a library up the road!' Another, departing bookless, won this epithet: 'Tight as a crab's arse!' I didn't escape: 'You don't have to buy a book every time you come over the door!' At Charlie's behest I began a series of pen drawings of Stromness closes and piers, printed by Wilfie Marr at Rendall's printing works. There followed a limited edition of eight prints of St Magnus Cathedral, published by Charlie Senior 'At the Sign of the Sea Horse'. Another of George's pals from Rose Street days, John Broom, episcopal priest-turned-librarian, and biographer of the communist revolutionary John Maclean, secured a job in Stromness Library. He engaged enthusiastically in amateur drama. He also assisted Charlie Senior, and on Charlie's sudden death took over the bookshop.

Another newcomer to Stromness was Tam MacPhail, husband of the artist and photographer Gunnie Moberg. He was soon working for John Broom, and on John's demise took over the running of what has been referred to as Scotland's only drive-in bookshop. Over the next forty years Tam became legendary. Chris Gauld remembers:

> The man behind the counter, tall, calm, greying, almost gaunt. Something of the night about him, hiding a kindness within.
>
> Near silent with a barely perceptible nod of hello, he'd quietly tap keys on a computer, listen to the children excitedly chatter, and let slip a smile.[1]

On Tam's death his friend and former assistant, Duncan McLean, remarked:

> He helped educate, entertain, and inspire several generations of Orcadians… he became a much-loved part of the Stromness community – so that when we lined Graham Place as the hearse went by, fishermen mixed with filmmakers, ministers with coalmen, dinner ladies with poets… Farewell Tam. And yes, I would like my book in a soundproof paper bag.[2]

[1] From *To the Memory of the Bookman*
[2] From 'Diary of a Shopkeeper', *The Orcadian,* 24 September 2020

6
A Visual Education

As a child I had gained much pleasure from drawing and painting, and a love of reading. Among the books that came my way, Charles Dickens' *David Copperfield* and the fantastic *Tales of the Arabian Nights* fed my imagination. The post-war availability of government grants opened the door for many to college and university, and more often than not, a career in teaching. Dead languages not being my strength, I failed university entrance. I was accepted by Gray's School of Art in Aberdeen.

'Digs' with Mrs Lewis at number 6 Belvidere Crescent meant a house full of students, two square meals a day and three at the weekends. Down Rosemount Place, past His Majesty's Theatre and the Art Gallery was the Art School, still occupying the building by the gateway to Robert Gordon's College. Among recent star graduates were Sylvia Wishart and Ola Gorie, with Ian Scott enjoying a postgraduate year in sculpture. Sylvia was already a prize winning landscape artist; Ola, under David Hodge, one of Scotland's leading silversmiths, was the college's first jewellery graduate. The distinguished Scottish painter Ian Fleming was head of the college; head of sculpture was Leo Clegg, who was also on 24-hour call as coxswain of Aberdeen lifeboat. A man of seriously left-wing views, he is thinly disguised as 'Theo', leader of Aberdeen's Communist Party, in John Aberdein's novel *Amande's Bed*.

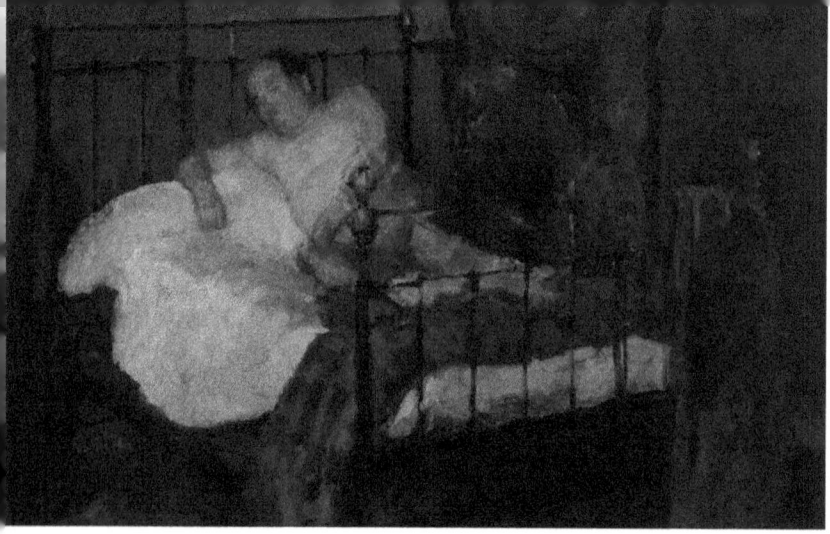

Jimmy Pickard poses for the Life Painting class

Drawing from the human form, and painting from plaster casts of classical sculptures, were still prized in the curriculum. The initial two-year Foundation Course was followed in my case by two years Drawing and Painting. Head of 'D & P', Henderson Blyth seemed sadly careworn. On a recent visit to the National Portrait Gallery of Scotland I was arrested by a fine self-portrait – a tin-hatted Henderson Blyth on the field of battle. Colin Thoms, a painter of mystical abstracts influenced by Klee and Miró, had during the war served in Orkney in the Army Education Corps. He would recount how his great-uncle, Sheriff Thoms, had bequeathed all his wealth to the restoration of St Magnus Cathedral, '... and all he left to us was his walking stick!' Among the lecturers was Frances Walker, who in her tenth decade is one of Scotland's most highly regarded living artists, awarded CBE for services to art.

At the weekends we headed for the Blue Lampie on the Gallowgate and Ma Cameron's on Little Belmont Street. In Holburn Street jazz was in full swing. After four years we went our individual creative ways. Among the graduates, Will Maclean from Inverness has become a leading Scottish artist; a 'Buchan loon' – Eddie Smith – makes exquisite model ships and boats; and Roberta Ratter, from Lerwick, married Dr Dawson Clubb to become the proud mother of six sons.

7

'Dis yer mither ken ye're workin'?'

After six months in Edinburgh at Moray House College of Education, I accepted the offer of a teaching post at Wick Academy. I was accompanied on the way back to my lodgings by a pupil from a travelling family. One day he asked: 'Dis yer mither ken ye're workin'? She'll be wantin' some o' yer paye!'

Wick was a fine town with many signs of former prosperity in the great days of the herring fishing, but my stay there was short lived. During the summer holidays I called past the Education Office in Kirkwall, and discovered a vacancy for an itinerant art teacher on a fortnightly rota of Westray, Sanday, Stronsay, Shapinsay, and no less than fourteen Mainland parish schools, many of them ripe for amalgamation.

My voyaging began with a crimson dawn and a calm sea on the early sailing of the *Earl Sigurd*, one of the last steam-powered vessels in Scotland. She called first at Stronsay to exchange cargo – and banter. The same sociable progress was repeated at Sanday and Eday and Papay, until we reached

An Orcadian Odyssey

Pierowall, Westray

Westray in the late afternoon, for me to spend a couple of days teaching at the schools of Pierowall and Skelwick.

Among the memorable people that I met in the North Isles was John D Mackay. 'John D' was a Papay man. Like others of his generation he had left school at fourteen, but the library of William Traill of Holland unlocked his intellect and spurred him, against the odds, to acquire an arts degree at Edinburgh University. From 1946 until his death in 1970 he served as headmaster of Sanday Central School. During this period he co-edited *The New Orkney Book*, and enlivened the letter page of *The Orcadian* with provocative wit, aimed at stemming 'the drift from the isles' and the erosion of local community powers. (From this would emerge the Back to Denmark movement, and indirectly, the establishment of Islands Councils for both Orkney and Shetland during the reorganisation of local government.)

'Dis yer mither ken ye're workin'?'

In the evenings, upstairs in his study amid piles of books and a great heap of unopened brown envelopes, 'John D' taught navigation to aspiring young fishermen. On one occasion Sandy Firth, itinerant teacher of technical subjects, was approached by John D. Would he care to visit the schoolhouse and solve a problem? The window of the study had been left open, and a sudden gust of wind had created a domino effect on the piles of books, ending up as an immovable heap against the study door. Sandy managed to prise the door open a couple of inches. Half an hour later, with the aid of a window pole he had managed to shift sufficient books to allow entry.

John D shared the schoolhouse with his housekeeper Hilda Meil, her husband Olie, and a cat called Chairman Meow. Hilda and Olie had been the last to live in the mansion of Geramount, before it was presented to the islanders as a community centre and lost its roof to a builder's merchant. On 'box' and fiddle they provided Sanday with a popular dance band. It was from Hilda in later years that I would acquire a rare photograph of the building of the Sanday United Presbyterian Kirk taken by John B Russell in 1881; and a fine oil painting, *The Earl Thorfinn in the Hurricane, 1953,* by her brother Douglas T Sinclair.

The most memorable voyage I had on 'the *Sigurd*' was returning from Sanday in a westerly gale. Against the wind with her propeller spinning in the air she made for shelter under Rousay, before turning with a carrying wind to Kirkwall – a four-hour excursion. About a year after I started, the island-hopping internal air service of Loganair came into being, making the itinerant life much more efficient, but no less colourful.

A daring young man

Jim Lee, the first pilot of the nine-seater Islander aircraft, was something of 'a daring young man in his flying machine', but is credited by many as the man who made

An Orcadian Odyssey

Innertoon, Stromness

the service work. On days of fog he flew only yards above the sea, then suddenly ascended over a misty shoreline to land on a grassy runway, often in a shower of coo sharn. On occasion, he flew on a level with the bridge of *Earl Sigurd*, giving the skipper a cheery wave. When several Russian 'klondyker' factory ships anchored within fishing limits, we were treated to a close inspection! After such adventures it seemed no big deal when as sole passenger heading home from Westray I was invited to sit beside the pilot. Once in the air, after some basic instruction he told me to make my own way to Kirkwall, and settled down to write up his log. I guided the aircraft with a diversion over Rousay all the way to Kirkwall, but didn't get to land it! After five years and some 600 passenger flights, I hung up my wings.

8

'Another bird that flew...'

Another bird that flew the itinerant nest was Howie Firth. Son of Stromness pharmacist and optician Nicol Firth, he had shown his mettle at Stromness Academy with a successful vote of No Confidence in the chair of the Debating Society. (No hard feelings.) We would share many escapades, among them in a time of burgeoning satire the Shopping Week *Late Night Review*, with colourful titles such as 'In Fae the Cuithes', 'The Warsiest Portions' and 'The Lovely Old Commode'.

Back to Denmark!

Howie graduated with First Class honours in Mathematical Physics from the University of Edinburgh, and carried out postgraduate research at Durham University where, like the Pied Piper of Hamelin, with his twin whistles he lured to Orkney the celebrated Northumbrian piper Kathryn Tickell and other fine folk musicians. He then joined the itinerant teachers serving North Isles schools. Biology lessons led to experiments in the shape of buckets and spades and a flourish of school gardens. When at Nicol Firth's fireside Sanday headmaster John D proposed the Back to Denmark movement, it was Howie who made it happen.

It was on a visit to Stromness in the summer of 1967 that John D Mackay threw an idea into the arena, then sat back amid smoke-rings to enjoy the stir. All the talk was of attempts by Harold Wilson's Labour Government to merge all Orkney's services under the umbrella of the Highlands and Islands, thus destroying Orkney's separate identity. Then there was much concern over the growth of unemployment, increased air and shipping fares and a low level of financial support from the new Highlands and Islands Development Board.

Recalling Orkney's former glory as an earldom under the Danish flag, John D suggested: 'Why not have a Back to Denmark Movement?' This appealed to a group of the young and energetic – students and others – and the Movement took off. A visit by the Secretary of State for Scotland, Willie Ross, was imminent. A 'mole' in the corridors of power ensured that wherever Ross went he was met by demonstrators and posters threatening a return to Danish rule. The Kirkwall councillor Edwin Eunson said: 'No doubt it will be considered a prank but at the same time it shows the underlying dissatisfaction in Orkney with Whitehall and St Andrew's House for the way they completely ignore our wishes and protests.' The county convener, Henry Willie Scarth, told Ross of the 'widespread feelings of resentment and frustration permeating the community'. Their progress under police guard to lunch at the convener's home, Skaill House in Sandwick, was halted at the gate by a sit-in of protestors.

In Stromness, there was particular resentment at the Government's failure to support new pier developments for the fishing industry. Here Ross was met by a mass of protest banners, including 'Willie Ross – Dead Loss'.

'Another bird that flew...'

Howie Firth

The St Andrew's Cross flew at half mast, but to crown it all Ross's route went past his effigy in straw hung by a noose from the freedom-fighter Alexander Graham's fountain at the Pier Head. Ross was seriously unamused, to the glee of the onlookers. A former schoolmaster, he dismissed the posters as 'the work of fourteen-year-olds'.

Soon, reporters from the national newspapers of Britain and Denmark converged on Orkney, and, during the summer recess of Parliament, emblazoned their broadsheets with tales of revolutionary fervour among the islanders. A box containing hundreds of their national flag arrived from sympathetic Danes.

Stromness Town Council responded by supporting a petition to the Queen asking for greater self-government and control. Another petition, signed by six thousand people, was handed in at 10 Downing Street by Jo Grimond MP, calling for the Prime Minister to make sure that any reorganisation of local government would allow Orkney to retain its own local authority. And this indeed was the case, eight years later.[1]

The Orkney Press

Howie left teaching in 1982 to take up the post of Senior Producer of the newly founded BBC Radio Orkney, and ventured into publishing. Along with Davy Sinclair ('Mr Flotta') I joined Howie and his wife Sidsel in The Orkney Press, to promote works on the history and culture of Orkney. Betsey I Skea (not to be confused with 'Country Woman' Bessie Skea) had been persuaded to record her reminiscences of life in Sanday. Would I illustrate the book? *Island Images*, replete with many tales and drawings, was published in 1982.

Others who would freely contribute illustrations to the Orkney Press were Jan Rouse, Anne (Leith) Brundle, Erlend Brown, Jim Baikie, Keith Laird and Isobel Gardner.

'Another bird that flew...'

The series *Aspects of Orkney* included W S Hewison's *This Great Harbour Scapa Flow*; *The People of Orkney* (a collection of a dozen or so essays by specialists on aspects of Orkney life); W P L Thomson's *Kelp Making in Orkney* and two volumes of *Old Orkney Trades* by Sheila Spence; *Symbol Stones of Scotland* by Anthony Jackson; David Sinclair's *Willick o' Pirliebraes* and *Willick and the Black, Black Oil*; Harry Berry's *The Driftwood Fiddle and other Stories*; *Orkney Short Stories*, celebrating the tercentenary of the Orkney Library; *Sea Haven: Stromness in the Orkney Islands* by Keith Allardyce and Bryce Wilson; *An Island Shore: The Life and Works of Robert Rendall* by Neil Dickson; *The Voldro's Nest and other Orkney Stories* by Margaret Headley; *Reading by Lamplight: Stories of Edinburgh, Orkney and Places in Between* by Rhoda Spence; *Lion's Heart* by Sissel Lie; *A Wild and Open Sea: The Story of the Pentland Firth* by James Miller; *Starfield: The Anthology of Science Fiction by Scottish Writers*, edited by Duncan Lunan. Then there were reprints of Orkney classics: Eric Linklater's *The Men of Ness*; R T Johnston's *Stenwick Days*; *Orkney Folklore & Sea Legends* by Walter Traill Dennison; Bessie Skea's *Island Journeys* and *Ancient Orkney Melodies* by David Balfour.

An Orcadian Odyssey

The Orkney International Science Festival

Never one to rest on his laurels, Howie in 1989 took up a contract with the City of Edinburgh to create a science festival, the first of its kind. He then returned to form the Orkney Science Festival. Initial puzzlement gave way to enthusiasm. The Orkney International Science Festival encompassed the study and enjoyment of all aspects of life, with attractions for all ages. Eminent speakers from around the world have graced the festival's stage, from Neil Armstrong, first man on the Moon, Dame Jane Goodall, zoologist and world expert on chimpanzees, to Nobel Prize-winner Professor Peter Higgs of 'Higgs Boson' fame. Maria Pia Casarini, polar historian and Director of the Instituto Geographico Polare Silvio Zavatti, and her husband Peter Wadhams, Professor of Ocean Physics in Cambridge and world authority on the parlous state of polar ice, regularly contribute. Along with Mr Boom, a happy intermix of music, song and dance, local food and drink and a score of enthusiastic volunteers and patrons, the Orkney International Science Festival has, with Howie at the helm, grown in stature and popularity, celebrating its 30th anniversary in 2020.

Admired and respected by all who knew her

Among the Science Festival enthusiasts was Thora Bain. Born and raised at the dairy farm of Saverock, as a young woman Thora was famously sacrificed on a pagan altar during the Octo-Centenial Pageant of St Magnus Cathedral. Having studied in Aberdeen at Craibstone College of Rural Domestic Economy, she spent her working life in Kirkwall running the Saverock Dairy on Junction Road. Deeply interested in the history and culture of Orkney, she had a remarkable recall for events and incidents and could hold an audience in thrall with tales of Orkney life. She was a founder of the Orkney

Thora Bain. Photograph © Selena Kusman

Heritage Society, and took active membership of many other groups. Into a great old age she rarely missed a lecture, and could be relied on for often intricate and lengthy comments. Howie said:

> We were very pleased to appoint Thora as our first Honorary Life Member as she encapsulated so much of what the Science Festival is about – taking a keen interest in the world about us, asking questions, and enjoying the search for new knowledge. She came to many talks and took a great interest in the festival, just as she did in any area of new ideas and insights.

On Thora's death, Sandy Firth, president of the Orkney Heritage Society, made this tribute:

> Thora was never afraid to express her opinion, or correct an untruth. Orkney has lost one of its most

endearing and hard working characters. Thora was admired and respected by all who knew her.

Howie's popularising format has given birth to science festivals around the globe. He has received an Honorary Doctorate from the Open University, an award of the Institute of Physics, and an MBE for services to popular science in the United Kingdom. He has lectured and written widely, including the substantial volume *Orkney* (Robert Hale, 2013).

1 *Stromness: A History*, pp 204–05

9

A Diversion

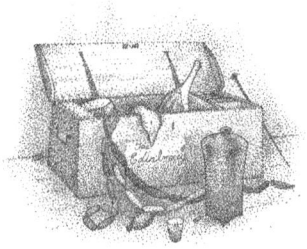

One day in Stromness some fifty years ago I met an old friend Tom Learmonth who asked, 'An whit aer thoo deuan wi theesel this days?' When I replied that I spent most of my spare time working in the museum, he retorted: 'Beuy, I thowt museums wis pieces whaur owld things cheust sat aboot on the shelves gaitheran dust.' Tom's impression was not short of the mark. Most of Britain's museums had been founded in the Victorian era. The Victorians' passion for scientific discovery led to the amassing and listing of all sorts of specimen collections: creatures of air, land and sea, rocks and plants from all over the world, artefact and costume of the world's richly varied humanity; archaeological specimens unearthed in an insatiable drive to discover the contents of every green mound. To house and display these collections, philanthropy and public subscription led to the founding of museums in towns and cities throughout the land. Many did not survive the demise of early enthusiasm, the lack of sustained funding and professional staffing.

An Orcadian Odyssey

Bryce Wilson, self-portrait

I had a little painting studio in Stromness at Quildon. One day early in 1971 there was a knock at the door. Johnny Pottinger, Honorary Curator of Stromness Museum, explained that an album of photographs of Stromness in Victorian times had been unearthed in London and sent north for inspection. The museum committee had arranged for the photographs to be copied and mounted by the local photographer Wilfie Marr. Would I be willing to set up an exhibition of the photographs? I hesitated, but a couple of weeks later Johnny returned and I agreed.

The unknown photographer had over a summer day recorded Stromness and its inhabitants. While much of the town of that time remains little altered, the people in the photographs reflect a different world. At Leask's corner, a woman delivers coal from a heather creel on her back. George Mackay Brown commented:

> In this fine collection of photographs, the town flows along from the South End to the North End like a sombre beautiful ballad... the peaky-faced barefoot children, the self-important Victorian merchants, the fishermen whose lives and livelihoods hung precariously on every wave and wind-airt. All are set in a seemingly changeless framework of Queen and Empire and Kirk.

The exhibition in the museum was intended to 'get feet over the door'. Stromness Museum was one of many throughout the country that had come into being on a wave of enthusiasm, and was one of the few that had survived. This was due greatly to the vision of the Reverend Charles Clouston, who was in 1837 a founder member of the Orkney Natural History Society. He would serve as Honorary President until his death half a century later. Under his guidance the museum eventually occupied a purpose built gallery above the Town Hall; from 1929 it owned the whole building.

An Orcadian Odyssey

STROMNESS

Late 19th Century Photographs

Revised with additions

Stromness Museum

Stromness folk had a fierce pride in their museum. The Town Council gave financial support, and each generation found time and skills to contribute. The natural history galleries were little altered from Victorian days – shelf upon shelf of preserved birds and mammals. In the years after the Second World War a start was made in providing habitat displays. A large mammal case was constructed, and Orkney's celebrated artist Stanley Cursiter, now living along the road at Stenigar, provided it with a shore scene

A Diversion

for the display of North Ronaldsay's seaweed-eating sheep – arguably his largest painting. Johnny Pottinger, who had drawn me into the museum to form an exhibition of photographs, soon had me assisting in a further project – a diorama of Orkney owls. Johnny had me well and truly 'hooked'.

I continued to research and arrange summer exhibitions. Probably the most successful from the 'feet over the door' point of view was *The Salving of the German Fleet* in 1974. Following a public appeal, many folk around Scapa Flow loaned items from the German Fleet, often acquired during the extraordinary feats of salvage carried out by Cox and Danks back in the '20s and '30s. The whole entrance gallery had to be cleared, display boards prepared and mounted, along with hugely enlarged photographs made directly from the glass plate negatives of Willie Hourston. An illustrated booklet was written by Johnny Pottinger. After months of preparation the exhibition opened in June 1974. Its popularity was such that space was cleared for a permanent display. Several years later the journalist Dan Van Der Vat paid a visit to Orkney. A wander through the streets of Stromness brought him to the museum:

> ...the museum [had] found room for a temporary display of pictures and relics... of the German ships sunk in Scapa Flow in 1919. It was so popular that it became permanent, and this is what I saw...

Van Der Vat's much reprinted book *The Grand Scuttle: The Sinking of the German Fleet at Scapa Flow in 1919* brought the sunken fleet to the notice of diving clubs around Britain and far beyond, founding a still flourishing recreational diving industry on the remaining wrecks in Scapa Flow.

The Lighthouses of Orkney (1975) involved a visit to 84 George Street, Edinburgh, headquarters of the

Northern Lighthouse Board. They kindly sent me home with an armful of original plans and drawings, and many photographs. When the Lighthouse Commissioners (the sheriffs of maritime counties) arrived in Stromness on their summer cruise they requested an evening visit to the museum. We dined regally on board NLB *Pharos*. Havana cigars circulated, followed by a tall silver cigar lighter in the form of Skerryvore Lighthouse. Thus suitably fortified and with crimson-lined capes fluttering in the wind, all the sheriffs of Scotland's maritime counties followed me up the street to the museum.

By this time I had been transferred from itinerant teaching to heading the Art Department of Stromness Academy. When Johnny Pottinger left Orkney I inherited the post of Honorary Curator. Then, when the Education Office planned to mark the centenary of state education in 1972, I was given the task of preparing an exhibition. Three years later, all public services came under the umbrella of the new Orkney Islands Council. From the old system of local government it inherited the site of a proposed farm museum in Harray, the existing Tankerness House Museum in Kirkwall, and financial aid for the Stromness Museum. Someone was required to manage and develop a Museums Service. After ten years of teaching, in November 1975 I embarked on a new career, as Museums Officer with Orkney Islands Council.

10

Oops!

No sooner had I relinquished teaching and begun to realise the enormity of the task before me, a recession and serious cut-backs put my new post in jeopardy. The council saved themselves the embarrassment of making me redundant, but made it clear that money was tight. I was based in Tankerness House Museum on the Broad Street of Kirkwall. This had been the spacious and elegant town house of the Baikies of Tankerness, one of Orkney's leading families, for more than three centuries.

With landowning in recession during the early decades of the 20th century, parts of the building were tenanted; then after the Second World War it was sold to the burgh council. Among those occupying the building at this time were the journalist and historian Bill Hewison with his wife, the painter Nancy Ramsay, and then by the artist Sylvia Wishart who had a studio there. There were those who pushed for Tankerness House to be demolished to make way for council housing, and even a car park, but wiser counsel prevailed and it was sensitively restored. The collections of the Orkney Antiquarian Society had for long been mothballed; they now formed the basis of Tankerness House Museum.

The little wood-panelled parlour from which many generations of Baikies had observed the busyness of Broad Street was now to be my office. A stone spiral stairway led to the former attic bedrooms. Here they had found a mouldering heap of leather-bound books. Having narrowly escaped being dumped in the Peerie Sea (at that time a convenient repository for, among other things, old sofas and mattresses), they had been dried out in the boiler room of the Education Office, then cleaned and polished by the museum custodian, John Windwick. The 500 and more volumes, dating from the 18th century, had belonged to the 7th laird of Tankerness, Robert Baikie, described as 'a polite, well informed, hospitable country gentleman'.

In the half-basement, archaeologists had exposed the original shore of the Oyce or Peerie Sea. Here were the remains of the ancient slipway where boats landed building stone for the construction of St Magnus Cathedral. There were chippings of red sandstone from the Head of Holland, and the dessicated remains of a Medieval leather shoe, now exhibited in the museum.

An archaeological repository of national significance

A six-week training period revealed an 'ivory tower' in the shape of the National Museum of Antiquities in Edinburgh. There I was assured by the director that artefacts of national importance would never be held by or loaned to a provincial museum. (And it has to be said, the rise and fall of museum projects in Orkney over a century and more had led many important Orkney artefacts to be placed securely in national and university museums in 'the sooth'.) However, with the appointment at Tankerness House Museum of curatorial staff, including Anne (Leith) Brundle as Assistant Curator, things were about to change. No longer did major archaeological collections automatically head 'sooth'. The Orkney Museum, as it is nowadays known, is an archaeological repository of national significance.

The enormous and ever-growing archaeology study collections of the Orkney Museum got shunted from one disused parish school to another. At last the former bowling rink beside the Kirkwall Power Station has been supplied with suitable conditions to meet modern standards of care and security.

A programme of summer and winter exhibitions came into being. The recently formed Scottish Museums Council regularly sent travelling exhibitions (the least popular being *Scotland Sober and Free*). The museum also prepared graphic displays, framed and boxed for transporting to island schools. (Before the days of computers and printers, temporary exhibitions employed Anne Brundle's skills in italic script, and the laborious use of transfer Letraset sheets.) With an alarm system installed, we were proud to receive a loan of original artefacts from the National Museum for a Viking exhibition that included part of the Skaill Hoard. (Overheard in the gallery: 'Why do they make these reproductions so big?') For a major exhibition of artefacts from Isbister Chambered Tomb we dreamt up the title *Tomb of the Eagles*. The archaeologist John Hedges used this crowd-puller as the title for his book, and it was adopted by the Simison family when they opened the restored tomb to the public.

Melsetter House, 1960s, © Sylvia Wishart

One of the finest of Arts and Crafts dwellings

At the end of the 19th century a wealthy Birmingham industrialist purchased the Melsetter Estate in Hoy. He set about rebuilding the ancient mansion of the Moodie family as one of the finest Arts and Crafts dwellings in Scotland.

Melsetter

Middlemore, Thomas, of Birmingham
Engaged William Richard
Lethaby to rebuild his island home.
So Lethaby
Entered the spirit of this place,
Turned stone & wood & glass
To light &
Enchantment, under a northern sky to
Rest & endure.

After the Second World War Melsetter House and farm were acquired by the Seatter family. They continued to welcome guests to enjoy the ambiance. The poet laureate Sir John Betjeman was fulsome in his praise for Mrs Seatter's pancakes, straight from the pan; while Charles, Prince of Wales, compared Melsetter House favourably with his granny's Castle of Mey over the Firth. For an exhibition to mark the house's centenary Elsie Seatter kindly loaned the pick of the furniture and other Arts and Crafts treasures. From the loft came spare ceiling panels of indigenous wild flowers by Ernest Gimson. All of this was packed up and conveyed across the Flow in J M F Groat's big van.

Serendipity

In a Museums Service on a shoestring it was all hands to the pump. The Custodian, Jim Park, revealed an extraordinary gift for model-making. Joyce Gray, appointed Clerical Assistant, developed and ran the School Loans Service. Tom Muir, appointed Assistant Custodian, had revealed a great interest in and knowledge of Orkney history and folklore. He researched an exhibition to mark the centenary of the death of the Sanday folklorist Walter Traill Dennison. We toured it to Sanday, and across the North Sea to Bergen University where Tom revealed extraordinary gifts as a storyteller. Having got the bit between his teeth, the following year he edited the works of Walter Traill Dennison, *Orkney Folklore & Sea Legends*, for The Orkney Press. Years later, when Tom served on an international team promoting the growth of tourism on the Viking Trail, he revived the art of storytelling at home and abroad. Tom has many books to his credit. He chairs the Orkney Storytelling Festival, and works as Outreach and Exhibition Officer for the Orkney Museums and Heritage. He and his wife Rhonda have founded Orkneyology.com, an expansive internet guide to the history and culture of Orkney, and Orkneyology

Press. In 2017 I joined them on a trip to Slovenia:

> This was Tom's fourth opportunity to fly the flag of Orcadian culture as guest of Ljubljana's long-established storytelling festival. On arrival Tom was whisked away for a television interview. Then his first talk was at the National Museum of Slovenia on the role of folk tales, an aspect of local culture too often neglected by interpreters of museum collections. The following day, in Ljubljana's splendid modern arts complex, Tom held a full house in thrall to 'Tales from Northern Shores'.
>
> The third day brought us to the University of Ljubljana, where in a crowded lecture theatre Tom delivered an illustrated talk on Orkney's prehistoric remains, bringing to life the dancing giants that form the Ring of Brodgar, and the Stane o' Quoybune that drinks at New Year from the Loch of Boardhouse (and woe betide anyone who witnesses this event).
>
> Formerly part of the Austro-Hungarian Empire, after the Second World War Slovenia became the northernmost part of Marshal Tito's relatively liberal Socialist Federal Republic of Yugoslavia. After his death in 1980 Slovenia strove for independence. In 1992 it was recognised by the European Union as an independent state, and later that year it was accepted as a member of the United Nations.
>
> Thanks to our friends Katarina and Dejan and Anja, we were treated to tours of this beautiful country. With a backdrop of the snow-clad Southern Alps we wandered the cobbled streets of ancient market towns, visited a vanishing lake and a castle in a cave, took a train-ride in the bowels of the earth among stalagmites and stalactites, and

Oops!

watched the sun go down over the Adriatic Sea.

    The last event of this visit was especially poignant, an evening of music and storytelling to celebrate the life of that late great Shetland storyteller Lawrence Tulloch, who along with Tom Muir had won enduring respect and affection in Slovenia.

An Orcadian Odyssey

A *ruckle o' owld stanes!*

The defunct Orkney County Council had made plans to form a farm museum. They had their eye on buying the historic farmhouse of Kirbuster in Birsay, but were disappointed when it fell into private hands. As a substitute, they purchased the ruins of Midhouse of Corrigall in Harray. This scheme did not win universal approval. Even the councillor for Harray dismissed it as 'noatheen bit a ruckle o' owld stanes!' And so things stood under the Orkney Islands Council. As part of my remit I collected farm and folk material here and there around the isles, against the day when the opportunity might arise to display them. Many disused farming and domestic items were donated by the people of Flotta, then transported by Bill Crichton of Occidental to storage on the Mainland. Ironically, in the barren days of the Thatcher era Job Creation Schemes were dreampt up to get young folk off the dole, and the creation of Corrigall Farm Museum fitted the bill. A team was assembled, and work began.

The plan inherited from the County Council was to recreate the traditional 'firehoose', with open hearth and neuk bed. Midhouse had originally taken this form, but upon examining the ruins we found that the stone gable inserted to replace the central hearth was still intact. The doorway leading through it from 'ootby' to 'inby' held a symbolic feature: a piece of the centuries-old single-stilted wooden plough, which had fallen into disuse, had become part of the door's lintel; and the neuk bed had disappeared in favour of the box bed. It was clear that the house should be restored to reflect those changes, a decision not appreciated by some!

While the buildings of Midhouse were being restored, another employment scheme, occupying part of the former Dounby Junior Secondary School and led by John Challoner, carefully repaired, restored and painted farm equipment.

Oops!

Tom Muir tells tales at Kirbuster

They built a replica of the South Isles ox-cart with four solid wooden wheels, copied from the last surviving example preserved in Edinburgh; and they wove a mile of heather simmon rope to clad the flagged roofs.

Over more than thirty years with peat stack, smoking lum, native sheep clambering over the roofs and ducks and hens pecking around the doors, dedicated custodians have given a warm welcome to hosts of appreciative visitors.

You'll likely ken what'll happen tae it when I'm gone.

Even a century ago, when motor vehicles were few and far between, on a Sunday afternoon a car might draw up at Kirbuster in Birsay. The Hay family had been a bit slow in adopting 19th century improvements. The old farmhouse was one of the few that still had a 'firehoose' and a neuk bed. In response to public interest they left things as they were, and so it remained until the last member of the Hay family moved out in the early 1960s. The farm went on the market and was bought by a Kirkwall businessman, the baker George Argo. Dated 1723, the old farmhouse has been described as the only unrestored survivor of its kind in northern Europe. George carefully repaired the roof, and stripped the pin-ups with which the walls had been decorated. Giving me a tour, George said: 'You'll likely ken what'll happen tae it when I'm gone.'

When George Argo died, in his memory the family offered to gift Kirbuster to the Orkney Islands Council. Since Corrigall had not been restored as originally envisaged 'to look as much like Kirbuster as possible', I was able to recommend acceptance as 'a feather in the cap'. Kirbuster filled the gap between Skarabrae and Midhouse of Corrigall in the Orkney story. At last the long history of the farming communities was well served, due to the generosity of folk throughout the islands.

The Naval History of Scapa Flow

As time passed the Council's Planning Department conceived a scheme to interpret the naval history of Scapa Flow at the Fuel Pumping Station in Lyness. The interpretation centre soon became a museum outwith the care of the Museums Service, a serious anomaly not redressed until the Museums Service came under the umbrella of the Planning Department. It was impossible to maintain suitable conditions for the well-being of many of the exhibits. (As I write a 'state of the art' building is under construction.)

With advice and assistance available from the Museums Service, the smaller islands began to develop their own interpretive centres, emphasising their individuality. When the 'Westray Stone' was discovered in Pierowall it was rushed to Tankerness House Museum before it could be spirited off to the National Museum as an artefact of national importance. It is now on loan to the Westray Heritage Centre.

11

This Town Shone

Stromness

So now we say that
This town shone when
Reefed sails rested
O'er pier & slipway,
Merchants prospered from
Needle to anchor, & an
Explorer ate his last landfast supper,
Sailed then to Arctic
Seas & an icy grave.

It has to be said that the town of Stromness had unlikely beginnings. Centuries before, folk had from time to time come ashore in Hamnavoe and headed up the brae:

Hellihole

Hard trodden, this steep path.
Even before the town's beginnings, pilgrims
Longing to dispel aches & sores
Landed here,
In hope of a cure at the
Haley Hole.
Over the centuries of Knox's cold dismissal, this belief
Lingered, then science claimed the well's
Essential virtue.

The heathery hill did little other than support a blazing beacon in times of danger. The rough and tumble of Brinkie's Brae did little for farmers, but it did provide the sheltered, if little used, anchorage of Hamnavoe. Kirkwall was the centre of power and commerce. Created a Royal Burgh with rights to foreign trade, it was from there that the landed families exported the produce of their estates to ports around the North Sea and the Baltic; but it was from those very ports that competing European states began to elbow for wealth and power on trade routes around and beyond the Atlantic Ocean:

> Avoiding the warring English Channel they increasingly took a northerly route and sought rest and repair in the village growing on Hamnavoe's western shore. The sheltered waters of Hamnavoe, and the neighbouring Cairston Roads, were thronged with ships from all over Europe, their crews eager for fresh water and provisions, and the pleasures of the tavern as they awaited a fair wind. The village grew rapidly.
> It was an age of raffish elegance. While merchants in panelled parlours sipped smuggled spirits, seamen

stumbled from inn to ale-house through foul closes. With the tinkling of a spinet, Miss Gordon lost her heart to a pirate. A trade war with Kirkwall was a lawyers' charter, but it gave Stromness a hero.[1]

One of those who prospered from the shipping trade was Bessie Millie, who ran her business from a hut high on the face of Brinkie's Brae:

Bessie Millie

Brave, the ship master who
Ever set
Sail without laying
Silver
In this withered palm.
Even the hardest, feigning jest, would
Make their way
Into her wind-blown lair,
Lest this Hecate
Lay tempest
In their path, sink their ship &
End their mortal day.

Many young Stromnessians were itching to go to sea,

among them John Renton, who ended up shipwrecked on a Pacific island:

John Renton

Just another lost to the
Ocean,
Hope long gone, but
Now, after seven years, a letter
Received, telling of his safe return.
Even his father did
Not know the lithe dark man who
Turned to greet him
On the pier, wearing a
Necklace of human teeth.

Another Stromness lad who made his name at sea was a totally different 'kettle of fish':

John Gow

Just across the harbour
On Garson shore stood the
House and garden of a respected merchant.
None foretold that his name would
Go down in infamy, when his son,
Outlawed for murder and piracy,
Was hanged in London – twice – at Wapping Dock.

John Login joined the navy as a surgeon, but made his name in India during the expansion of the British Empire:

Sir John Login

Son of a ship-owning merchant &
Innkeeper who hosted sea captains &
Rigged their craft with well-water,
John was destined for higher things.
Over many years as a surgeon in India,
His sterling qualities were
Noted & he became guardian to the child Duleep Singh,
Lahore's deposed maharaja & Victoria's protégé.
On Login's early death a
Grateful queen chose the memorial stone,
Inscribed 'The memory of the just is blessed' to honour his
Name.

My remit included giving 'what assistance I could' to Stromness Museum, where I was still Honorary Curator. To avoid competition, an agreed Collecting Policy reserved archaeology, rural life and industries to the care of the Museums Service, and maritime and natural history chiefly to Stromness Museum.

In the 1980s we had a visit from Dale Idiens, Keeper of World Collections at the Royal Museum of Scotland. She examined Stromness Museum's Pacific Collections, and concluded that the 18th century pole spears must have arrived here in Captain James Cook's ships, *Discovery* and *Resolution,* otherwise 'How on earth would they have got here?' Cook's ships had dropped anchor in Stromness in June 1780:

Discovery & Resolution

Driven north by summer storms,
In Cairston Roads the
Ships now rested. All the talk was of
Captain Cook,
Of his violent death on a Pacific shore, his ships
Venturing north to Bering Strait, south &
East to the Atlantic,
Returning after four years,
Yearning for landfall
& loved ones.
Round the tables of the town, William Bligh
Enthralled his listeners (George
Stewart would later sail with him
On 'Bounty', & drown in chains on 'Pandora',
London-bound on a charge of mutiny).
Unable to pay crew intent on
Tavern & alehouse, they
Invited the viewing & purchase
Of exotic souvenirs – conch horns, clubs & spears
    from southern seas –
Now to be treasured on a northern isle.

Dale Idiens also noted the collections relating to the Hudson's Bay Company, and in particular those concerning the distinguished Arctic explorer Dr John Rae. On Rae's death in 1893 his widow Catherine had donated his portrait, his surveying octant, his hunting gun and his snow goggles. From other sources came his powder horn, his 'state of the art' inflatable dinghy, and the fiddle used to promote dancing as exercise during the dark Arctic winters.

Erebus & Terror

Even in John Franklin's sixtieth year,
Relentless pursuit of the
Empire's applause
Brooked no qualm.
Under Jane's persistent clamour, he was
Sent to seek
& sail in triumph the North West Passage.
The ships lay moored in Stromness Harbour, only
    two islanders
Engaged as crew. Franklin dined ashore with Margaret
Rae, whose son John would survive the
Rigours of Arctic exploration, solve the mystery
Of Franklin's disappearance, & discover
Rae Strait, vital link in a North West Passage.

It is well known that Franklin's widow Jane did her best to erase the memory of Rae's achievements in favour of those of her husband, who had died with all his party while seeking the Northwest Passage. Franklin appears in bronze in both hemispheres, and even in Stromness there is 'Franklin Road'. The tide began to turn in the 1980s with the appearance of Robert L Richards' biography *Dr John Rae*, bringing meat to the bone of the explorer's life and achievements.

No Ordinary Journey

Dale Idiens at John Rae's grave, 1993

Dale Idiens' proposal for a centenary exhibition in the Royal Museum of Scotland came to fruition in collaboration with Tankerness House Museum and Stromness Museum. *No Ordinary Journey: Dr John Rae Arctic Explorer 1813–1893*, opened with fanfare in Edinburgh, and after three months, in Kirkwall at Tankerness House Museum. The original intention to tour the exhibition in Canada did not prove practical; the illustrated text panels found a permanent home in Stromness Museum.

Passage

John Walker, an acclaimed Canadian filmmaker, brought the tale of John Rae to our television screens. Filmed in Orkney and Canada, *Passage* finished with a discussion panel held at Admiralty House in London. Among those taking part were Tom Muir from the Orkney Museum, Tagak Curley, political leader of the Inuit community that reported to John Rae the fate of the Franklin expedition,

Tagak Curley and Gerald Dickens

and the actor Gerald Charles Dickens. We witnessed an historic moment when Gerald Dickens apologised for the words of his great-great-grandfather Charles Dickens – 'The word of a savage is not to be taken for it'. The apology was graciously accepted by Tagak Curley on behalf of the Inuit community.

The Canadian writer who has in recent years brought the Rae story to a popular readership is Ken McGoogan, with the widely read *Fatal Passage* and *Lady Franklin's Revenge*. At long last Dr John Rae, thanks to that formidable lobbyist Margaret Street, received a Blue Plaque on his retirement dwelling at 4 Lower Addison Gardens, Holland Park, London. There followed posthumous membership of the Royal Society of Chartered Surveyors, a life-size bronze statue at Stromness Pier Head, and a carved stone plaque in Westminster Abbey, albeit at the feet of Sir John Franklin! Finally, he was awarded posthumous Freedom of Orkney. The John Rae Society has purchased Rae's birthplace, the Hall of Clestrain, to restore the building in his memory.

An Orcadian Odyssey

The Staigs of Innertoon, Stromness

An incomparable colourist and master printmaker

One evening in September 2016 Tom Muir opened his door to a woman with a bottle and a mission. Dr Barbara Rae CBE RA RSA, Scottish painter and printmaker of international repute, was to take her third cruise on the Northwest Passage. Tom was persuaded to embark as guest speaker. Barbara Rae recalls:

> Drawing anything out of doors means working fast before your fingers freeze. I had to ditch the warm palette I used for Spanish and Irish works and concentrate on colder colours with a predominance of deep Prussian blues and coloured blacks. There is so much unexpected colour in glaciers, icebergs and icecaps – strong manganese blues and water a deep indigo. Evening skies were a painter's heaven: strips of pink, orange and yellow set against indigo seas. The ice has a blue-green underside, a strange contrast from the brilliant white top surface and black water.[2]

This Town Shone

Sea Ice – Ilulissat © Barbara Rae

In 2018 the exhibition *Barbara Rae, The Northwest Passage*, filled the magnificent Royal Scottish Academy in Edinburgh, the Pier Arts Centre in Stromness and Canada House in London. At the grand opening in Edinburgh Tom addressed the guests on *John Rae: A Man of Two Worlds*. His essay also featured in the lavishly illustrated hardback

An Orcadian Odyssey

Barbara Rae and Tom Muir in the Northwest Passage
Photo © Caro Mantell

catalogue published by the Royal Academy of Arts and dedicated to Rae's memory. The artist, learning that she would feature in *An Orcadian Odyssey*, responded: 'So long as you make me glamorous.'

Barbara Rae

1 *Sea Haven: Stromness in the Orkney Islands*
2 Exhibition Catalogue, *Barbara Rae, The Northwest Passage*

12
'He came home'

A friend and neighbour, Ethel Young, had taught around the globe before returning to Orkney to pursue a dedicated career in primary schools. She indulged her enjoyment of the natural world through membership of the Orkney Field Club, and photography, often from the Park, her much-loved cottage in Rackwick.

In Stromness, Ethel noted that the inscriptions on gravestones were often vulnerable to decay. She led a dedicated group in recording and publishing the inscriptions in *The Kirkyards of Stromness and Graemsay*. Among the families of merchants and mariners, farmers and fishermen, the stones too often record early death and losses at sea. Particularly poignant is the one for the Arctic whaler James Taylor who was a victim of the disastrous whaling season of 1835, and his brother George:

> A token of respect to the mem[ory] of JAMES TAYLOR who, after passing through great suffering, d[ied] at sea 1835, 3 days before ship reached home, and GEORGE TAYLOR, a lov[ed] brother, who was drowned in the Thames 1851.

Among the many gravestones was one that had been erected by a certain G S McTavish for friends 'as a mark of regard for their care & kindness during his boyhood'. The adjacent stone was inscribed:

> In mem[ory] of my beloved husband GEORGE SIMPSON MCTAVISH b[orn] in Rupertsland Canada 13 Feb[ruary] 1863, d[ied] in Victoria, British Columbia, 30 Apr[il] 1943. He came home.

Intrigued, I consulted the Stromness census returns. For 1871, among the eight people registered 'from Hudson's Bay' four were at school, and one of them was 'George McTavish, boarder, scholar, aged 7'. He lodged in Alfred Street with Isabella Jobson, whose sister Cecilia Hourston taught in the Subscription School at the foot of Hellihole. The middle name of 'Simpson' led to consulting James Raffan's biography *Emperor of the North*. Long before achieving that title a young Highlander named George Simpson had left school in Dingwall, Inverness-shire, for apprenticeship with his uncle's sugar brokerage in London. He took to business like a duck to water and, as an eligible bachelor, succeeded in fathering two daughters by as many mothers.

With the advance of the 19th century competition in the fur trade between the Hudson's Bay Company and the North West Company led to outright warfare. Back at head office in London, the directors of the HBC 'head-hunted' the 'bright young broker' George Simpson to set sail for Rupert's Land and sort things out as Overseas Governor. His infant daughters, Maria and Isabella, he sent to the care of relatives in Dingwall. Both would grow up there and marry, but Maria and her lawyer husband Donald McTavish were particularly favoured. The couple received from Governor Simpson the sum of £500, enabling them to emigrate with their son, George Simpson McTavish, and set up business in Rupert's Land.

As the Governor's grandson, George rose through

York boat, Orcadian design

the ranks of the Hudson's Bay Company to the lofty position of Inspecting Chief Factor. A pattern had emerged among HBC officers of bringing their often mixed-blood children to be educated in Orkney. It was George Simpson McTavish's son – and namesake – who at a tender age was brought across the Atlantic for schooling in Stromness.

Among the many private schools that existed in Stromness before the Education Act of 1872 was the Subscription School, founded at the foot of Hellihole by a group of fee-paying families. The teacher Cecilia Hourston displayed her credentials through publishing a book of poems, *A Teacher's Offering*. One of her pupils, John Oman, became a distinguished theologian, rising to be Professor of Systematic Theology in Cambridge. He recalled: 'Miss Hourston gave me her book of poems... I still retain some memory of the multiplication table which she drilled into me...'

Clearly Isabella Jobson and her sister Cecilia Hourston provided the family care that George Simpson McTavish, great-grandson of Sir George Simpson, had left behind in Rupert's Land. There was at that time no possibility of 'going home for the holidays'. After long years in Stromness George returned to Canada to follow the 'onwards and upwards' path beaten by relatives of the 'Little Emperor'. Having risen to the rank of Chief Factor, he attended the company's 250th anniversary celebrations. On retirement in Vancouver Island he wrote his reminiscences. Through the World Wide Web I located in a second-hand bookshop in New York a rare first edition of his autobiography, *Behind the Palisades*.[1] Within the week it fell through my letterbox, and I read:

> I, GEORGE SIMPSON McTAVISH left school in Stromness, Orkney Islands, shortly after my 15th birthday, and joined the good ship 'Prince of Wales', which belonged to the Hudson's Bay Company, and sailed for Moose Factory, James Bay, the southern part of Hudson's Bay.

There followed a fascinatingly detailed account of life in the Hudson's Bay Company, initially as a junior clerk at York Factory, a major point of arrival and departure of the Hudson's Bay Company ships. The trading post was run on a military discipline:

> When the bell in the belfry tolled the midday dinner hour, we assembled in the mess room – and each person had his appointed place. At the head of the long table stood Mr John Fortesque, Chief Factor in charge, opposite him at the foot, Mr John K. McDonald as 'Second', while guests and officers ranged behind their chairs on each side. A large oil painting of Sir George Simpson, famous Governor of the Hudson's Bay Company in Canada, hung on the wall. When all was ready Grace was said, chairs drawn back, and everybody seated themselves.

He Came Home

YORK FACTORY

Strict rules were applied to food supplies and other necessities: 'each officer had yearly allowances of tea, flour, sugar and other essentials...' In the fall of the year a good supply of fish was netted and spread out to freeze for the long winter months:

> The chief mainstay in our food was venison, salt geese and white-fish. Occasionally we had beef when it was considered advisable to kill an old ox. With duck, ptarmigan, plover and other feathered game we fared very well, though the greatest want was in vegetables... turnips were grown for their tops, as root vegetables did not develop to any extent. Preserved (dry) imported vegetables were most often used in soups, and Edwards desiccated potatoes in tins, fourteen pounds and over, really was our standby as an antiscorbutic, when salt geese, salt beef or pork had to be relied on... With mallards for dinner, a whole duck was deposited on a plate, and often like Oliver Twist, we came back for more.

Beaver and an occasional young polar bear when

roasted added very acceptably to a variation of diet. The lake white-fish were of inestimable quality, and when fried we never got tired of them, but the small river white-fish were, especially when simply boiled, and out of condition, ofttimes anything but palatable, even with Hudson's Bay sauce – hunger.

The swamps afforded a goodly variety of berries, and the mess allowance of sugar went largely in the making of jam, raspberry, yellow or eye-berry and cranberries... Eggs were cheap in those days, and cost a shilling a dozen... Almost all our private supplies were received from and through Stromness... and all eggs received were packed in fairly fine salt... the quantity of eggs imported... rather astonished me and in 1880 we had two hundred and fifty dozen in the guardroom alone. These eggs naturally augmented our cuisine, only instead of considering them as a breakfast food, they were eaten at night in our intermittent refreshments... at York Factory we fared better... than the interior or isolated posts... at [Fort] Churchill, for example, we were on the verge of hunger many a time, and had to conserve every ounce and morsel of food...

George Simpson McTavish

McTavish goes on to say:

Each officer had a yearly contract with an Indian washerwoman, the wives of the men who had settled and married... Mrs Sally Gunn was assigned to me... and contracted to do my washing, mending, making moccasins, mittens, leggings, ornamented with beads or silk, or anything necessary... during the years I was at York Factory, Sally never neglected me... I shall always feel Sally's debtor.

'Waste not, want not' was the name of the game. 'No nails in boxes, strap iron round cases, wood, paper or sacking were thrown away in our days of active and constant need. Everything was made straight, mended and treasured'. Even a century ago, McTavish could write: 'Waste is the crime of this age, and prodigal indifference is calamitous.'

'The natives come down from Nelson River to trade... this fort sends home 7,000 to 33,000 made beaver in furs, etc., and a small quantity of white whale oil.' In return the Company traded firearms and ammunition, knives, colourful blankets and dress materials, tea and tobacco. A welcome break in the dark and frozen winter was the Christmas holiday, 'a whole week's nightly rioting of the light fantastic till New Year's Day':

> The dresses of the Indian men and women brightened up the dim candle-lit interior, the women in various patterned and coloured printed-cotton dresses, beautifully wrought silk and beadwork moccasins... with bandana silk handkerchiefs for headgear. The men had on capotes [long hooded coats] of white and black duffle... fine blue-cloth with gilt buttons. Gaudy... sashes girded their loins, while beaded or silk wrought caps of tanned deerskin adorned their heads. On the feet and legs, moccasins tanned, smoked or in plain white, in fancy-coloured silk-worked designs and beaded leggings with ornamental garters... Our men... sported silk flower-wrought deerskin shirts or coats... when the room warmed up, and the sweat began to trickle down the walls... superfluous clothing were discarded. Their shirts clung... tightly and wetly to the men's backs... No mincing steps... could fit in with the racing tunes that halfbreeds, Indian or white musicians extracted from their fiddles... it was a whirlwind of vitality and speed!... The stoves glowed red with intense heat... Women's suffrage... conceded the right to choose their own partners... [all] had to give their best in Red River jigs, Scotch reels, the Rabbit, Duck dances

and the Old Dan Tucker... the only safe place for recuperation was on a snow bank outside with 40 degrees below zero... With only a couple of hours in which to have a cold tub and sleep before breakfast, we left an experience of unalloyed happiness no-one could forget. So ended my first Christmas at York Factory in 1879.

George Simpson McTavish experienced the whole gamut of HBC life, from clerking and hunting, fishing and trapping to the administrative heights of Chief Trader. Among those with whom he worked was Ouligbuck, son and namesake of Dr John Rae's interpreter during the discovery of the fate of Franklin. McTavish describes him:

'Buck' impressed me as being a man of intelligence... he had acquired a phonetic perfection of language... with an enhanced vocabulary,

William Ouligbuck

therefore it was a treat to converse with him...
He could talk his own language, Chipewyan, Cree
and English... He could do blacksmith work with
the ingenuity of his patient people, was tinsmith,
carpenter, sledmaker, hunter, trapper, boatman,
could splice a rope and make a net, was respectful,
and could be a 'white' man with the dignity of a
trained mind. And yet he was Esquimaux, could eat
raw meat with the rest of his confreres, and could
[on occasion] forget the luxuries of the forts...

In Stromness with his wife in September 1926 George McTavish erected a gravestone for the Hourstons. In his autobiography he remarked:

The richest woman I knew was a lone spinster
who taught children – myself among them – their
A, B, C, and laid with sometimes heavy hand on
our small anatomies and seats of true learning the
foundations of understanding. We all shared her
love. She was found dead alone in her little two-
roomed cottage, leaving a heritage that... directed
many a one the straight path through life...

After his death in 1943 George Simpson McTavish's widow brought his ashes to rest beside Isabella and Cecilia: 'He came home.'

---

1 A soft-back reprint of *Behind the Palisades* can be purchased on the Internet.

13

Points of View from Across the Atlantic

From the beginning of the 18th century the London-based Hudson's Bay Company made Stromness a recruiting point. For nigh on two centuries Orcadians would engage in the fur trade, founding families among the First Nations people of Rupert's Land around the Bay.

In 1980 the Canadian Broadcasting Corporation made a film of two Cree fiddlers from James Bay. They were Bob McLeod and Ray Spencer, who was descended from William Sinclair of Eastabist, Harray and his Cree wife Nahoway. They visited Orkney to compare tunes with local fiddlers. To their delight the Orkney fiddlers heard familiar tunes, but played in the style brought to Rupert's Land by Orcadians and Scots centuries before.

The research of Dr Patricia McCormack of the Provincial Museum of Alberta would lead to a revival of links between Orcadians and their mixed-blood cousins. In 1984, researching family ties, she spent some weeks in Orkney, meeting Mary Bichan and others and recording their stories. We paid a visit to Ken and Alice King for a gourmet supper and tales of Alice's grandfather and granduncles in the Hudson's Bay Company. As a result of all this I accepted an invitation to give an illustrated talk at the 5th North American Fur Trade Conference, held by the Lake St. Louis Historical Society in Montreal. In her letter of invitation the secretary remarked:

> Never before have previous conferences thought to seek points of view from across the Atlantic. Quite frankly, I think that hearing from someone such as yourself will enhance not only the conference but the knowledge of the delegates.

The five-day conference encompassed some seventy twenty-minute illustrated presentations, among them 'The Orkneymen and the Hudson's Bay Company'. This was the catalyst of a series of presentations by Orcadians in Canada over the following decade and more.

Northwind Dreaming

The importance of the Hudson's Bay Company's Fort Chipewyan as Alberta's earliest permanently settled community would be recognised by a major exhibition and conference in Edmonton, opened in September 1988. *Northwind Dreaming* was the result of three years' research by Dr Patricia McCormack. It would portray the daily lives of the people who had made Fort Chipewyan their home over the past two centuries, including First Nation, Metis (mixed-blood) and non-native people.

Tankerness House Museum contributed to *Northwind Dreaming* the sort of personal items, such as his fiddle and his Bible, that a young Orcadian might have brought with him to Rupert's Land. A small group of Orcadians, Ethel Young, Alice King and myself took up the invitation to attend the exhibition and conference in late September 1988. Dale Idiens gave an illustrated talk: 'John Rae,

1813–1893: Explorer and Ethnographer'. I made a slide presentation: 'The Orcadians in the Canadian Fur Trade', portraying the background that made Orkneymen so well suited to the work of the Hudson's Bay Company, and stressing Orkney's living links with Fort Chipewyan and other HBC outposts, through the Metis descendants of the Orkneymen. There was already talk of holding the Colloquium of the Rupertsland Research Centre in Stromness in 1990. Dale Idiens now proposed that we work together to mark the centenary of the death of Dr John Rae in 1993.

Following the two day *Northwind Dreaming* conference delegates boarded a chartered 'Dakota' aircraft for a 1¼ hour flight and a day out at Fort Chipewyan. (Patricia McCormack, Alice King and I stayed on for three.) 'Fort Chip' was beautifully situated on Lake Athabasca at the edge of Wood Buffalo National Park, a vast area teeming with wildlife including the largest free-roaming herd

Fort Chipewyan, Lake Athabasca

Points of View from Across the Atlantic

of bison in the world. The settlement grew up around the Hudson's Bay Company trading post, occupying a strategic position in the waterways connecting the inland fur producing areas with York Factory on Hudson's Bay. The community of trappers and workers that had grown around it, and the Catholic and Anglican missions established there in the 19th century, consisted of Cree and Chipewyan First Nation, French and Scots Metis and a small white community. The Scots Metis were chiefly descended from Orcadians; Louttits and Wylies and Fletts. (One Cree woman assured me that 'Flett' was purely a Cree name, nothing to do with Scotland or this Orkney that I kept going on about!)

We visited Horace Wylie, retired hunter and trapper, whose grandfather William Wylie joined the Company from South Ronaldsay in 1862. Horace's mixed-blood mother was granddaughter of Colin Fraser of Assynt, celebrated piper to Governor Sir George Simpson. On his bookshelf were *The Orkneyinga Saga* and *Reminiscences of an Orkney Parish*. He had an impressive collection of snowshoes, beaded husky blankets and other First Nation memorabilia, now displayed in the 'Fort Chip' museum.

Horace Wylie shows his First Nation collection

Horace recalled that he had sent food packages each Christmas to his cousins in Orkney. When he paid a visit in the 1960s, he was surprised at how advanced Orcadians

An Orcadian Odyssey

Horace Wylie (2nd from left) and his sister visit their Orkney cousins, 1970s

were, having been brought up on his grandfather's tales of central hearths and neuk beds. Between his lakeside home and the shore stood a wooden sundial, a replica of the one erected in 'Fort Chip' by Sir John Franklin, on his way to explore the Arctic coastline in 1820. And it was in 'Fort Chip' that a Graemsay man, John Ritch, built the boats *Castor* and *Pollux* and *Goliath* for the Arctic explorers Dease and Simpson, on their expedition of 1836–39.

We met Roderick Flett whose father had come from Orkney in the late 19th century. Roderick's son Lloyd 'Sonny' Flett was president of the Fort Chipewyan Metis Local which handled community affairs along with the Cree and Chipewyan First Nation Bands. Far from the sea, Fort Chipewyan enjoyed extremes of climate – hot in summer, when it was only accessible by air or water; minus 40°F in winter, when a 200km frozen road connected with Fort Mackay in the south.

Points of View from Across the Atlantic

Despite the contrasts, Fort Chipewyan had some surprising similarities to Stromness. It was on approximately the same latitude, built on the same granite shield, and came into existence through water-born trade. It had a population of around 1,500, and a fishermen's co-operative. Since the decline of the fur trade in the postwar years the community had had to seek new forms of employment. Some fur trapping was still carried on by licensed hunters, who were also allowed to hunt moose and caribou for their own consumption. Income could be augmented by the manufacture of traditional beaded footwear and clothing, at which the First Nation and Metis women were highly skilled. Fishing, in the past a subsistence occupation, was now carried on commercially. The original clinker-built fishing skiffs were believed to be an adaptation of the Orkney yole, but flat bottomed to accommodate the shallows of Lake Athabasca. The fishermen, who supplied 'walleye' (pickerel) for freezing and export by their local co-operative, the Delta Native Fishermen's Association, used skiffs of plywood or aluminium, with outboard motors. We visited Carl Granath, manager of the fishermen's co-operative, and his wife Elsie. We supped on fried moose, cranberry pie and blueberry cake. (Another hospitable household produced caribou stroganoff, blueberries and cream.) Carl then showed us photographs of his trap line, and proudly displayed fox and beaver pelts.

Since 1978 many Fort Chipewyans had found employment some 170 miles away with Synecrude of Fort McMurray, where oil is extracted from the Tar Sands. A new development at 'Fort Chip' was a pilot scheme for the extraction of Canadian Shield granite, which when polished made an attractive cladding for buildings.

My diary recalls:

> Dan Greurer took Alice and me on a high speed trip in his aluminium skiff, first out into the Bay which

is not more than 5 ft deep in this area, then we landed on English Island where Nottingham House, the first HBC fort, was established by Peter Fiddler. This was a peaceful and lovely place, the sun shining through yellowing aspen and shimmering on distant waterways. The shores were piled high with whitened driftwood, sometimes whole trunks of trees – an Orkney beachcomber's dream. All around marshland plants have grown up on the mud flats, exposed now since an up-river dam lowered the level of Lake Athabasca – English Island is no longer an island. We then took a turn into the beginning of a waterway which connects with the Arctic…

The Wood Buffalo National Park attracted several hundred visitors annually. In 1987 the community completed the Fort Chipewyan Tourist Lodge, a ten bedroom hotel with a superb view over Lake Athabasca. Nearby, a replica of one of the demolished Fort buildings was being constructed as a museum. Fort Chipewyan also sported a community hall and curling rink, and a well stocked 'Bay' store. The beautiful Athabasca Delta Community School was opened in 1986, and at Keyano College young adults could learn work and business skills. We discussed with the headmaster the possibility of a school visit to Orkney. At Keyano College I took the opportunity to show slides of Orkney to young adults and senior pupils. They showed a keen interest. How did we exist without snow to make winter roads, or trees with which to construct buildings? I showed them St Magnus Cathedral.

Before leaving 'Fort Chip' we were showered with gifts. Alice was given an HBC copper trade pot and miniature moccasins. I received a history of Fort Chipewyan, a miniature mukluk, and a leg trap from a trap line at Sandy Point, used by Louttits and Fletts some forty years before.

Points of View from Across the Atlantic

A school visit to Orkney

'Fort Chip' pupils at Tomb of the Eagles with Ronnie Simison

The following year, after a major fundraising effort a school visit to Orkney came to pass. Senior pupils spent a week in Scotland followed by a week in Orkney, where they enjoyed the hospitality of families around Stromness. Dallas Clarke wrote:

> I think this was a great idea as we got to understand how people lived over there. Kurtis and I stayed with John and Fiona Cumming and their two sons, Grant, 18, and Sean, 16. We had a great time with them. During one evening John and Grant took Kurtis and I kayaking. It was our first time in a kayak but they said we were very fast learners. We had fun playing soccer, volleyball, badminton, basketball and finished with an hour of swimming. For me, the highlight of the day was the basketball game. We played against the

students of the Stromness Academy and won handily 22-10.

The Folk Festival being in full swing, the Chipewyan party performed square dancing at the Pier Arts Centre. Horace Wylie's grandson Rodney Marten visited his cousin Bob Wylie in Holm; Kurtis traced his distant relative Willie Mowatt in South Ronaldsay. Rodney Marten wrote:

> ...we were on our way to Stromness. There were people there to greet us, and a bag piper played for us!!!! Man, it was great! Everyone kept staring at us; we had the floor, man!!!! While we were in Stromness we went touring. We got to see a lot of grave sites, like the Tomb of the Eagles, and stuff like that. I must say it was fun!!
> Would you believe that I met a distant relative, Bob Wylie. I didn't feel comfortable at first but Lynn and Maureen were there and that helped a lot. 'Thanks, guys.' It was so funny because they were so white, and believe me, I ain't no sack of flower!!! 'HA HA'. Someday you should try some Scotch Whiskey and potato chips.
> There was this Folk Festival going on and we got to do some square dancing. The music player for some reason couldn't get the right song to play. Could you imagine all these people waiting there for the square dancers from Canada to perform!!! 'Man, what a laugh.' You know, I never realized that I liked Folk before!!
> On the Orkney Isles, out of all the islands, they have only one forest, and when I saw it I burst out laughing. I mean, really now, it was so small. Then I heard that it was planted! Man, that just about killed me. You see, I wasn't used to seeing and hearing things like that. Like I'm from Canada where we are trying to get rid of our forests to build roads and

Points of View from Across the Atlantic

Len Wilson with Dan Stephen, Cree fiddler and trapper, Fort Selkirk, May 1994

stuff. We should take a look at Scotland and see just what might happen to us.

Well, it was time to come home, and we all said our good-byes, and shed a few tears. Then it was on to the ferry (I never knew that I got sea-sick, maybe because I had never been on an ocean before! HA HA HA!)

It was nice to get home, but that is one trip that will stay with me forever!!!!!

A bit of advice – if you ever travel to Scotland, you have to get to try Haggis and Black Pudding!!!!!!!!!!!

All and all the trip was great!!!!!!!!!!!!!

P. S. THE BREWING DISTILLERIES WERE TOTALLY NARLY, MAN.

The following year, Horace Wylie sent transcriptions of letters written by both his father William Wylie and his Orkney relatives. Alexander Wylie wrote from the croft of Newcastle in Burray in 1897, to John Wylie in Fort Chipewyan:

An Orcadian Odyssey

Duncan's Boatyard, Burray

Dear Nephew,

This is the first time I have wrote to you… I was so glad to hear from you all. So we wish you all a very Merry Christmas and a Happy New Year… The Christmas was pretty dull here and very little sport at the baa [Burray], the day was so stormy. So the young men and girls had a dance in the hall at night. They kept up the dancing till three o'clock in the morning. There was a ball on New Years night, the tickets was 2 shillings a pair…

  There was a couple got married short ago in the south parish Ronaldsay, old John Duncan he was 77 years of age and his bride 27, so I will not give up hopes yet. I hope that you will take a look to Orkney sometime yet if all is well and take a wife from Orkney that I have the pleasure of being at the wedding. If you were here in the summer time I don't think that you would go back again, the country is so pretty with all nice lassies and flowers growing and then the beautiful shell sand at the sea shore. The fishing time is very lightsome, they are going to built a new pier in Burray now, she is to be something over 200 feet long and 40 feet wide...

Rupert's Land Colloquium, Stromness, Orkney June 1–8, 1990

The cream of historians and archivists from North America and Scotland joined their Orkney associates in the Stromness Hotel for a week of presentations and site visits. Local speakers were William P L Thomson (Kirkwall Grammar School): 'Sober and Tractable? The Hudson's Bay men in their Orkney Context'; James Troup (Stromness Academy): 'The Impact of the "Nor Wast" upon Stromness'; and Bryce Wilson (Orkney Museums Service): 'The Hudson's Bay Collection in Stromness Museum'.

Of the visiting academics, Dale Idiens of the National Museums of Scotland contributed 'Dr. John Rae, 1813–1893: Explorer and Ethnographer'; C. Stuart Houston of the University of Saskatchewan: 'Dr John Rae, the Most Efficient Arctic Explorer'; John S Nicks of Cultural Resources, Toronto: 'William Tomison and his Peers in Orkney and Hudson's Bay'; and H Lloyd Keith of Shoreline Community College, Seattle: 'A Return to Scotland: Hudson's Bay Company Fur traders in Retirement, 1843–51'.

Orkney's former North American territories

The inclusion of Orkney in the discussion of fur trade history seemed almost to have become standard practice. In May 1994, with the support of Orkney Islands Council five from Orkney made presentations in Edmonton at the Rupert's Land Colloquium held in the University of Alberta. There was Alice King with 'Tales from the Attic: Letters Home from the Watt Brothers'; Katrina Mainland

(Kirbuster Museum) with 'The Traditional Country Background of the Orkney Mainlander Recruited by the HBC'; Jim Troup with 'The Parish of Orphir 1821'; Len Wilson with 'Fiddling in the Fur Trade: the Influence of Scots/Orcadian Music'; and Bryce Wilson with 'Orkney Influences on John Rae, Arctic Explorer'.

Beside the city of Edmonton was a full-sized replica of the original Fort Edmonton founded by William Tomison in 1795. Joining us there at the end of Colloquium barbeque were blacksmith Willie Mowatt MBE and his wife Maggie, from Governor Tomison's native parish of Burwick in South Ronaldsay.

The published *Proceedings of the Rupert's Land Colloquium* included my account of the bus tours:

> The bus tours which sandwiched the Colloquium gave a rare opportunity, especially for the Scottish participants, to visit fur trade sites and soak up the history of the Canadian province of Alberta. There was also the chance to meet old acquaintances and to make new ones, before and after the three days of the Colloquium.

Rocky Mountain House – Jasper Bus Tour

On Monday 23rd May we set off westward, past the 'nodding donkeys' of oil-rich Alberta to the town of Rocky Mountain House and the Walking Eagle Motor Inn. Fed and watered we spent the afternoon at the National Historic Site, under the guidance of Ross MacDonald. At the time of building in the early autumn of 1799 the North West Company's Rocky Mountain House was the most westerly fur trade post, but within weeks it was competing with the Hudson's Bay Company, whose Acton House was built within a stone's throw (and by all accounts stones were thrown, with an amicable truce at the Festive Season).

Points of View from Across the Atlantic

Until the merger of the companies in 1821 the two forts competed fiercely for the trade of Kootenay and Blackfoot. The Hudson's Bay Company continued to trade there until 1875 in a succession of buildings, one of which was burnt to the ground in 1868.

The Rocky Mountain House site was also important as the base for the explorations of David Thomson and others in the shaping of modern Canada. Today, the National Historic Site protects 228 hectares of pleasant unspoilt landscape by the North Sackatchewan River. While little of the original structure remains, careful site interpretation is introduced in the Visitor Centre and continues on the fort sites with the reconstruction of base planking and, here and there, audio stations with illustrations and recorded messages telling the stories of early days at Rocky Mountain House. A fur press, a Red River cart and a York Boat punctuate the trail.

Many of the party who later ventured forth in the warm evening air spent a memorable hour in the town's Rocky Mountain House Museum. Here the ample portrayal of the social history of the area in a series of home and work sessions was enhanced by Duke's eloquence and his virtuoso performance on the pianola (appreciation of which was later given proper expression among the malts of the Walking Eagle Motor Inn).

Next day revealed the scenic highlights of the tour. Bighorn sheep posed on rocky outcrops and trod the verge of the highway as Orcadians, accustomed to low horizons, were spellbound by the massifes of Banff and Jasper National Parks.

Our first stop was at Saskatchewan Crossing with a view of the approaches to the Howse Pass, traversed by David Thomson in 1807, which brought the fur trade west of the Rocky Mountains. Then at the Columbian ice fields we saw from a distance the toe of the great Athabasca Glacier. A packed lunch was consumed with relish at vantage points around the Sunwapta Falls, with the sun filtering through tall pines and ravens nesting precariously above the roaring waters of the gorge. Later, at Athabasca Falls, cameras clicked over the 'thundering spectacle' of the Athabasca River squeezing through an improbably narrow canyon of quartz-rich rock.

Arriving at Jasper's Marmot Lodge in the mid-afternoon provided a welcome rest period before a walk around the town with our tireless tour escort, Bill Yeo. Here we noted similarities to towns in the Scottish Highlands, including some fine granite buildings. (Most of the party then opted for an early night, leaving pursuit of the elusive malt to the indefatigable few.)

The homeward journey brought us through Pocahontas, where we explored the preserved site of Jasper Park Collieries, established in 1908 to service Canada's growing industries and railways (we hoped for a glimpse of a bear). Having enjoyed a picnic lunch in Edson Centennial Park we were warmly welcomed at the town's Red Brick Arts Centre and Museum, and shown with pride its recently completed theatre.

With the Colloquium and its myriad impressions behind us, we bade farewell to stalwart friends and set off on the long haul to Peace River in the far north of Alberta. The sign on the bus read 'V.I.P. PARTY' so it was no surprise to find the inhabitants of St Albert lining the sidewalks three deep and responding gratefully to our gracious hand waves, only to discover that they were anticipating the carnival procession coming up behind, led in a snowy shower by a bikini-clad Miss St Albert reclining gracefully on the hood of a smart limousine.

As we passed through mile upon mile of farmland and forest Adèle Boucher detailed the development of

Albertan settlement and the present state of the economy. Many fine old farm buildings survive, but some are slowly sinking into the earth (a stream of photocopies passed around the bus showed us the state of pioneering life a century ago).

At River Flats, Athabasca, hub of the northwest fur trade in the 19th century, we enjoyed the first of several welcome meals and refreshments graciously served by community groups along the route. Here also we had a close-up view of soon-to-be-demolished wooden grain silos – one of which may be preserved as an historic site.

Onward we travelled, through Gruard, scene in 1899 of the signing of Treaty 8, to Donnelly, where colonists from Québec first settled in 1912. There we visited the first Francophone church, and were served coffee in the church hall.

Farther north the plains gave way to rising ground, till at last we were looking out over a broad panorama of the town of Peace River at the junction of the Peace and Smoky rivers, highway of fur traders and Arctic explorers. (This spot also housed the grave and monument of Twelve Foot Davis, whose twelve foot gold claim financed the trading ventures that helped develop the district.)

From our base at the Peace Valley Inn we paid an evening visit to the Peace River Centennial Museum which has excellent fur trade displays. (Here I learned the current trading rate: one beaver pelt = one bottle of Highland Park single malt.)

The following day we took a meandering route west and south, exploring the great farmlands of northern Alberta settled over the past century: the Shaftsbury Settlement, the region's first major farming operation, by John Gough Brick, in 1889; Old Wives Lake, site of the first Shaftsbury farm in 1883, and stopping place between Peace River and Dunvegan.

At Friedenstahl we were treated to coffee and buns by the Westphalian Roman Catholic community who settled the area in 1912. (Beside the community hall was an extensive display of tractors and steam engines and other farm equipment which kept cameras clicking for the benefit of Orkney Vintage Club.)

Onward we sped past the intriguingly named 'Highland Park' where many immigrants settled from Eastern Europe in the 1930s, and Hine's Creek, site of the mass grave of Beaver Indians who died in the 'flu pandemic of 1918. Thence to Fort Dunvegan which, founded for the North West Company by Archibald Norman Macleod in 1805, remained an important landing and crossing point of the Peace River into the 20th century. The site includes a fine new interpretation centre. To my surprise I came upon an imagined portrait of William Tomison,[1] the Orcadian inland governor of the HBC. A guided walk included many historic buildings. Here was the Factor's House, built of squared logs in 1877–78, and furnished in period. Anglican and Oblate Missions were established as the century progressed, and by 1914 hostelries for travellers had been built on both sides of the river, but the promotion of Dunvegan as a future city came to naught when it was bypassed by the railway. (In this fertile river valley, market gardens are farmed just as they were a century ago.)

Replete from the picnic lunch enjoyed at Dunvegan, we continued south on a convoluted route past the sites of early homesteads at the Peace River Prairie and the Heart Valley, including the Hudson's Bay Company Ranch of 1888. On through Valhalla, colonised by Norwegian Lutherans (who else?) in 1912, we skirted Lake Saskatoon in quest of trumpeter swans and finally reached Grande Prairie, 'first city of the Peace River Country', to spend the night in the Grande Prairie Inn (where the bar closed at 9pm).

In the evening, those with sufficient 'get up and go' were rewarded by a tour of the Pioneer Museum. Here we viewed the rare white moose, and much travelled Dawson Bar, a relic of the Yukon Gold Rush. The Pioneer Village contained original houses and stores and other

Points of View from Across the Atlantic

early buildings collected together as a permanent record of the not-so-distant past.

Next day, the final leg of our journey brought us to Saskatoon Mountain. Besides the 1950s radar base and the archaeological dig of the region's earliest known settlement we had a rare view westward across the vast plain to the distant white-peaked Rockies.

Our last lunch stop was at the town of Sexsmith, 'Grain Capital of the British Empire'. An excellent buffet was served in the community hall, and lapel badges were added to our growing collection. A walk around this pleasant town revealed the preservation of many fine buildings from the '20s and '30s (this was also the opportunity for some to buy last-minute souvenirs).

The long afternoon run to Edmonton took us over the fossil-rich Kleskun Hills and through Glenleslie, site of a Pre-World War One community, past Sturgeon Lake Reserve and the site of Fort Assiniboine, the early 19th century fur trade post.

At last we entered Edmonton, where here and there fellow travellers left the bus to a chorus of fond farewells. Finally, the remnants of the party were deposited, tired but happy, in the warm evening sun by Lister Hall. For the Orcadian party and many more, the Colloquium and its tours were a memorable experience and a further strengthening of historic ties.

In a letter to the OIC Convener Hugh Halcro-Johnston, the chairman of the Rupert's Land Colloquium Conference Michael Payne had this to say:

> Overall I suspect that Orkney could not have picked a better or more knowledgeable group of goodwill ambassadors to send to Canada... The opportunity to have Bryce and Len Wilson, James Troup, Alice King and Katrina Mainland at the Colloquium helped make it a memorable event for all participants – almost as memorable in fact as the Colloquium

held in Orkney… Len Wilson's Music Night was a rousing success. Over 300 people attended the evening, which was also taped for a brief news report on the CBC radio network which serves all of the North West Territories and the Yukon. In addition, Alice King was interviewed about her remarkable collection of family letters by CBC for their morning radio show… I hope this will prove the start of even closer personal and professional ties between Orkney and what sometimes seems like Orkney's former North American territories.

Ties would indeed be maintained. In 2004, Cree dancers, singers and storytellers spent eight days in Orkney. Many took advantage of the 'homecomings' of 1999 and 2007; the Foden (Twatt) family of Kirkwall became honorary members of Sturgeon Lake First Nation and in 2005, along with representatives of Orkney Islands Council, attended the annual Sturgeon Lake Pow Wow. But with the financial crash of 2008, culture was sacrificed to save the banks.

First Nation dancers, Tankerness House Gardens, Homecoming 2004

Points of View from Across the Atlantic

The following obituary appeared in the *Rupert's Land Newsletter*, Fall 1998:

In Memoriam Alice and Ken King, Stromness, Orkney

(We regret to report the deaths of Ken King in the spring of 1998 and of his wife, Alice, during the summer. Their friend and fellow Rupert's Land member, Bryce Wilson, has kindly provided the following notice for the newsletter.)

The community of Stromness in Orkney has been saddened this year by the deaths of Alice and Ken King. Alice's family, the Watts, had a strong connection with the Hudson's Bay Company; in the mid-19th century her grandfather and grand-uncles served the company in clerical and administrative posts.

Alice and Ken made several visits to Canada to visit relatives and attend conferences. In 1988 Alice attended *Northwind Dreaming*, the bicentennial exhibition and conference of Fort Chipewyan in Edmonton, and spent several days at Fort Chipewyan. When letters from her grandfather and grand-uncles were found in the attic of the family home, Alice with the help of her daughter Zelda had the letters transcribed and made a vivid presentation based on them, 'Tales from the Attic', at the Rupert's Land Colloquium in Edmonton in 1994. Two years later she and Ken attended the Rupert's Land Colloquium in Whitehorse and made an expedition to Inuvik.

Ken supported Alice's interests with a friendly and helpful presence. Their home, 'Holmlavoe', built by Alice's grand-uncle Chief Factor William Henry Watt in the 1870s, was a place of warm hospitality for many Canadian visitors.

An Orcadian Odyssey

Tom Muir

1 The portrait of Tomison looked familiar. I later discovered that it was based on a photograph that Dr Patricia McCormack of the Museum of Alberta had taken of Tom Muir.

14

'Not bad, for a Shapinsay lad'

From time to time at the Orkney Museum I would receive a visit from a dapper Orcadian exile, keen to discuss the furnishings and exhibits of the Baikie Rooms. It was in the secondary department of Stromness Academy that I had first encountered William Mowat Thomson[1] – 'Billy Ballet' – working briefly as an itinerant teacher. He had grown up near Balfour Castle in Shapinsay. His father was gardener there, and the castle spurred his love of 'the finer things'.

William Mowat Thomson

As he grew William blossomed in athletics and the performing arts. Spotted in Kirkwall by a ballet teacher, he studied in Edinburgh and London, paying his way by piano accompaniment. He returned to Orkney to teach.

Morag MacInnes remembers how he reassured the only boy at the ballet class in Stromness Temperance Hall:

Some young men, he said, were very silly about ballet, and thought it was a girlish thing to do. This, it seemed, was all wrong. The boys had twice the responsibility of the girls; they had to be immensely powerful, and graceful as well. Without a man to lift her, he said, a prima ballerina would look like nothing, tittupping about the stage ... If Christopher kept up his practice, then, when he was bigger, the ballet man said, he would be like a fine, strong tree holding up a bright red apple.[2]

Artists from around the world, among them David Bowie

Returning to Edinburgh, William went from strength to strength. With the encouragement and business acumen of his friend Noelle, Countess of Mayo, in Shandwick Place he started the first full-time dance course in Scotland, and won the contract to teach schoolchildren throughout Edinburgh. As time passed he founded a second venue, this time in St Stephen Street, Stockbridge, known as the Theatre School of Dance and Drama. In addition to local children and adults, his reputation was such that he welcomed artists from around the world, among them David Bowie, the actor Stephen Berkoff, and the dancer Lindsay Kemp.

By the year 2000 William had succeeded both culturally and financially, and could indulge his love of 'the finer things'. He bought an Adam castle on the Borders, and ended up in a magnificent house on Edinburgh's St Bernard's Crescent. 'Many describe his vibrant hosting of dinner parties and gatherings, picturing him at his grand piano surrounded by paintings, furniture and collectibles that would be the envy of any museum.'[3]

I last saw William in July 2019 when I visited 19 St Bernard's Crescent along with his cousin Tom Muir and Tom's wife Rhonda. Now in his mid-eighties he showed us around the house with undiminished enthusiasm. Among the extraordinary treasures he indicated a Louis Quinze sofa, saying, 'And there, sat the Duchess of Argyll. They tell me I can't take it all with me, but I'm doing my best!'

Sadly, later that year on 8th October, William died of a heart attack, but not before cancelling an appointment to provide piano accompaniment to a dance class. The *Scotsman* obituarist had this to say:

> Mowat Thomson touched the lives of everyone he met. Sometimes that meant helping a lost soul find their way or encourage a talented but wayward dancer to focus and strive; at other times it meant renting out the basement flat of his gorgeous home on St Bernard's Crescent to touring performers such as Barbara Windsor or Christopher Biggins. The Edinburgh dance world may have lost a giant, but his legacy lives on in every plié and pirouette executed in classes across the city. Mowat Thomson leaves behind a thriving scene that he helped to shape and grow, and indelible memories in everyone who learned from him, laughed with him and dined at his table.[4]

Not bad, for a Shapinsay lad.

1 William Mowat Thomson 8 April 1933 – 8 October 2019
2 Morag MacInnes, *The Ballet Man*
3/4 Obituary: Kelly Apter, *The Scotsman*, 4 November 2019

Above: Croval, Sandwick
Below: Instabilie, Quoyloo

15

Margaret Gardiner & the Pier Arts Centre

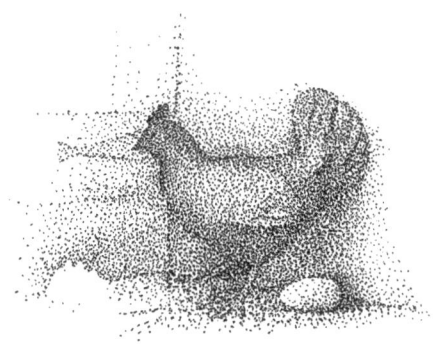

Sylvia Wishart arrived one day at Sunnybrae, breath on lip: 'I have met a woman from London who plans to give to Orkney a collection of paintings and sculptures by major figures of contemporary art!' I had not had long to absorb this extraordinary turn of events before a knock came to my office door at Tankerness House, and here was the woman in question – Margaret Gardiner. She had, she explained, for many years passed her summers in Rousay, and now in appreciation she intended to gift many works of the St Ives school, among them those of her close friends Barbara Hepworth and Ben Nicholson. She was planning to set up a charitable trust to hold the works for the enjoyment of the people of Orkney. Would I care to become a trustee?

It is worth saying at this point that Margaret Gardiner's grandfather, a successful businessman in the City of

London, had left his progeny sufficiently endowed to provide a private income, with the stricture that they put it to good use. They did him proud. Margaret's father, Sir Alan Gardiner, was a distinguished hieroglyphist, and one of the first to enter the tomb of Tutankhamun. Her uncle, Balfour Gardiner, has been described as 'one of the most significant composers of his generation'; her nephew, Sir John Eliot Gardiner, is a conductor of world repute, and founder of the Monteverdi Choir. Margaret was herself a founder member of the Institute of Contemporary Arts, a political activist in the face of Nazism and the Cold War, and an active member of Amnesty International. She represented the International Federation for Disarmament and Peace at the World Congress of Peace Forces in Moscow, October 1973.

The first informal get-together of this 'gang of three' – Margaret Gardiner, Sylvia and me – took place in the Graemsay manse. Margaret explained that she had purchased many of the works to support her friends during their early struggles; others had been given to her in their years of fame and prosperity. Now in her early seventies she looked to their future. Her son Martin Bernal had no wish to live in a house full of valuable works of art. Tate Britain would have happily taken them off her hands, but a lifelong altruism won the day. Back in the '50s Margaret, having by chance taken a holiday with her son in Orkney, lighted on and bought an abandoned cottage in Rousay. As time passed she became aware that among the islanders many potential artists had little chance to view important works of art 'in the flesh'.

Margaret Gardiner soon discovered that making such a gift would be an up-hill battle, both from a conceptual and a monetary point of view. She was determined that the works be freely available, in a place that was inviting and easily accessible. A friend, Jim Ede, had opened a gallery in Cambridge, Kettle's Yard, showing similar works in a domestic setting. When Margaret had visited

Margaret Gardiner & the Pier Arts Centre

Sylvia Wishart in Stromness she had seen the potential. Sylvia lived down a close near the Pier Head in the former store and pier of J A Shearer, General Merchant. Redolent of the days of sail, the pier and store had served Shearer's coastal trading vessels, the coopers and curers of the herring fishery, a coal store, and for some thirty years the employment agency of the Hudson's Bay Company. During the Second World War it was the headquarters of the Royal Engineers. Now Sylvia, seeking seclusion to get on with her work, was willing to sell; and the adjacent dwelling fronting the street might also be on the market.

The appointment of trustees and patrons, along with the complexities of raising capital and revenue funding, both local and national, fell heavily upon the shoulders of Margaret Gardiner. She approached many possible donors. The whole scheme might well have fallen through but for the completion of the Occidental Oil Terminal on Flotta. At the opening ceremony early in 1977, among other gifts to the people of Orkney Dr Armand Hammer announced £50,000 towards the Pier Arts Centre project.

With Margaret Gardiner and Neil Firth, director of the Pier Arts Centre, at Margaret's 90th birthday party

To this the Orkney Islands Council added £10,000.

The complexities and setbacks of acquiring the buildings, appointing architect and building contractor, trustees and patrons, were at last overcome. Revenue funding was secured from the Scottish Arts Council and Occidental Oil Inc. Beginning with Tate Britain, the art works made a stately progress northward via several major public galleries until at last, under the curatorship of Erlend Brown, with Marjorie Linklater chairing the management committee, on 4th July 1979, 'with a great flourish on a blazing, beautiful and hot day',[1] the Pier Arts Centre was opened to the public.

Margaret Gardiner had masterminded the whole exercise, down to the positioning of the last work of art on the gallery wall. The strain had taken its toll, almost leading to a nervous breakdown. She was awarded OBE for her services to art. Throughout the rest of a long life she was preoccupied with the financial wellbeing of the Pier, and regularly attended meetings. I would collect her off the plane, sometimes on a stormy winter night. All the way to Stromness she recounted her trials and tribulations, then at Heatherybraes (Sylvia's house), with a blazing fire and a glass of claret, conviviality reigned.

Swartafiold was the name of the Rousay croft, high on the steeps of Sourin. Margaret had grown very fond of the island and its inhabitants. 'I was Rousay's first white settler', was her rueful comment. The light of neighbouring Fa'doon sometimes burned late. 'We were reading.' said Jimmy. 'One wouldn't find that in a country district of England,' said Margaret. Her son Martin Bernal brought his wife and children for summer holidays:

> The kids loved being there ... as Robert Burns expressed it in Auld lang Syne, they would run 'aboot the braes'. Jimmy's grandchildren were often at Fa'doon, and the two gangs would fight battles

Fa'doon, June 03

Fa'doon from Swartfield

between England and Scotland... I would take my children to different parts of the island: to a little 'geo', or inlet, by Midhowe; to the sea by the lake of Wasbister; or up the hill to the lochs in the middle of the island.[2]

An Orcadian Odyssey

The parlour, Swartafiold, with works by Nicholson, Hepworth and Wishart

In the kitchen of Swartafiold hung an Alfred Wallis. In the parlour, a screenprinted fabric by Barbara Hepworth shared space with a painting, 'Tree of Birds' by Scottie Wilson, and a view of her Rackwick window by Sylvia Wishart. On the floor were rugs designed and woven by Nicholson and Hepworth. In her bedroom hung 'Grandmother's Bed', a drawing by a young Eduardo Paolozzi who had for a time occupied the little summer house of 35 Downshire Hill, Margaret's Hampstead home.

Margaret was no mean writer, and Swartafiold provided the necessary peace and quiet. Having completed the monumental task of creating the Pier Arts Centre, she had time to reflect on her life and times. Her first book, *Barbara Hepworth: A Memoir*, was published in 1982. As a student in Cambridge she had formed a close relationship with Bernard Deacon, a promising anthropologist. While on a study visit to Malekula in the South Pacific island group of Vanuatu (formerly the New Hebrides), Bernard Deacon, still in his early twenties, had died of blackwater fever. He had been held in such high regard by the community in which he had lived and worked that some sixty years after the event, knowing that Deacon had had 'a special friend, a woman', they had traced Margaret. During a trip to Australia in 1983, she fulfilled the invitation to visit Malekula. Later that year we lunched in Kirkwall at the Lynnfield Hotel. Amid the murmur at surrounding tables Margaret described her visit to Malekula; how the women wore grass skirts, while the men 'wore only penis sheathes': a sudden silence. The following year in Edinburgh the Salamander Press published *Footprints on Malekula: A Memoir of Bernard Deacon*.

A Scatter of Memories was dedicated to her 'gaggle' of grandchildren. The Foreword relates:

> Throughout a life that spans the century Margaret Gardiner has known some of the most distinguished artistic, literary and scientific figures of our time. In *A Scatter of Memories* – a fascinating mix of autobiography, reminiscence, political reportage and short stories – she gives us new and memorable insights into D. H. Laurence, W. H. Auden and Louis MacNeice, among others.
>
> Also included is her widely admired memoir of the sculptor Barbara Hepworth, and her own account of how she gradually built up a collection of modern paintings and sculpture... The book opens with a conversation in which she speaks of her background; her experience of progressive education and of Cambridge in the early decades of the century; and the anti-war activity that has been a lifelong concern – from anti-fascism in the 1930s, through to the Vietnam War and disarmament campaigns of the post-war period.
>
> Described as having 'a genius for friendship', Margaret Gardiner is also someone who has been 'involved' throughout her life. Both qualities are

amply reflected in this elegant and moving work.

Margaret Gardiner is also the author of *Footprints on Malekula: A Memoir of Bernard Deacon* ... and the subject of a Channel Four documentary, *Time is a Country: The Memories and Friends of Margaret Gardiner*.

No longer fit to wander the hills

My mother once declared that she feared nothing and nobody. Margaret could frequently be 'out of order' at committee meetings, and was treated, in my view, with undue deference. It was my turn to take the chair. I took Mum's advice, 'Let her off with nothing.' After the meeting Margaret and I went for a G&T at the Royal, and a cup of tea at Sunnybrae. 'Bryce bullies me,' said Margaret. 'I expect you deserve it,' replied Mum. 'Milk and sugar?'

Margaret Gardiner & the Pier Arts Centre

By this time Margaret was no longer fit to wander the hills and crags of Rousay, or to swim in the rock pools, although she still swam early each morning among the ducks and coots in the Ladies' Pond of Hampstead Heath: 'They break the ice for me in winter.' She had concluded that she must with great reluctance relinquish Swartafiold.

One evening at Sylvia's table: 'What will I do with it? If I sell it, the English will buy it. And besides, what would I do with the money?' She turned to me: 'Would you like it Bryce?' I spent many holidays there over the next quarter century, wandering the hills and crags of Rousay and finding the peace to get on with writing and drawing. I served on the Pier Arts Centre Trust for eighteen years, the final seven as chairman.

Margaret's son Martin recalled:

> On her death in 2005 at the age of 100, I received many condolence letters and cards from Orkney. Two Orcadians, Neil Firth, the director of the centre, and Bryce Wilson, an artist and museum curator and a long-term friend and ally, gave moving speeches at her memorial meeting in the Institute of Contemporary Arts in London. The Pier Arts Centre is now flourishing and expanding.[3]

Among those attending the memorial meeting was the distinguished left-wing intellectual and former leader of the Labour Party, Michael Foot.

Martin Bernal had studied modern Chinese political history and was for nearly thirty years a Professor of Government and Near Eastern Studies in the United States, at Cornell University. His three volume *Black Athena,* on the Afroasiatic roots of classical civilisation, provoked international controversy. He was a founding trustee of the Pier Arts Centre. His son William cut the cake at the Pier's 40th anniversary celebration on 14th July 2019.

An Orcadian Odyssey

When she handed over Swartafiold, Margaret Gardiner expressed the hope that from time to time I might make the house available to artists. Among those who took up the offer were the land sculptor Richard Long (now 'Sir') with his wife Betsy; the painter and print-maker Erlend Brown; and the photographer Keith Allardyce Hobbs. In '96 Margaret King from Lancashire enjoyed five weeks of summer. Her diary records:

> ... after doing these sketches, I decided to walk as far as I could towards Faraclett, especially as the beginning of the walk would be in the lee of Swartafiold and out of the West Wind. I love this land, so being careful of the oystercatcher's nest, I set off over the stile; there is a point beyond which the giant skuas will not let me go, and one flew right at me. I did not have a stick, so I shot up my arm and shouted at him to Clear Off and he did! I stayed still and he went away and sat on top of the cliffs.

Margaret King held an exhibition of fine flower studies in Tankerness House Museum. She wrote:

> I was born in St Annes-on-Sea where there were sandhills in the middle of the town, as well as all along the shore. The harmony of this land beside the sea has inspired me all my life... Gales upheave the sea-bed and fling all sorts of things high up on the beach in a tide-line which catches the sand and helps the flowers and grasses to grow and dunes develop. The Evening Primrose blooms at mid-summer, this lovely flower is thought to be from America and could have come to these shores with cotton bound for the Lancashire cotton mills on ships which sometimes foundered on this coast. I think that to be aware of the connectedness of

everything is vitally important.

Margaret King sent copies of William Shakespeare's *The Tempest* and *A Midsummer Night's Dream* for the library of Swartafiold:

Margaret

Midsummer Night's Dream
At Swartafiold, where I
Run the gauntlet of a thousand bonxies,
Gaze on a hundred unsetting suns
And sing with the seals in the caves of Faraclett.
Rivers of light dispel the night, while
Even the star watcher sleeps, dreaming of
The Tempest of Jupiter.

Now in her ninth decade, Margaret King is preparing for an exhibition in Lytham St Annes. Another visitor to Swartafiold was the Icelandic photographer and writer Thorgrimur Gestsson, researching a guide to Orkney and Shetland:

Thorgrimur Gestsson's voyages in Orkney,
in the year Two Thousand & Eight

Egil Bragi,[4] gold-scatterer,
to the word weaver of Iceland
offered grape & barley & legend.
Then Thor's helmet guard
rode wind & tide,
stood swordless in Sigurd's Wirk,
broke bread with Cubbie Roo, &
by the kirk of the murdered earl
washed his feet
in the skull-cleaver's wake.

Orkney Islands Council possesses an extensive

collection of Orkney art, both donated and purchased in times of plenty. The works are displayed in public places around the islands – schools and libraries, museums, community and heritage centres, Orkney College – but never together. Inevitably, many rarely see the light of day. Among our northern neighbours – Norway, Faroe, Iceland – there are galleries that give an overview of local art, an essential barometer of the health and cultural wealth of the community. Someday perhaps, in the not too distant future, this gap will be filled by an Orkney Gallery.

Bog Marigolds, Rousay by Margaret King

1/2/3 *Geography of a Life* by Martin Bernal, Xlibris Corporation 2012
4 Egil Bragi = Tom Muir

16

Tales to Dine Out On

1

A hot day, St Anne-on-Sea. Sketchbook in hand, Margaret King buys an Italian ice cream:

'Oh how lovely, you are an artist! I don't paint... but there's cousin Eduardo of course, he's a sculptor.'[1]

2

5th November 1936. At the door of Number 15 Well Park, Stromness:

George Mackay Brown: 'A penny tae burn me Pop!'
Cathie Wilson: 'Georgie Broon, you're far too big to be going with your Pop!'

3

7th July 2006. An elegant octogenarian at the door of Swartafiold, Rousay:

'I am Felicitas Vogler. I was married to Ben Nicholson, and I knew Margaret Gardiner. I have a retrospective of my photographs at the Scottish National Gallery of Modern

Art, and I am in Orkney to arrange for an exhibition at the Pier Arts Centre. May I come in?'

Sadly, Felicitas Vogler died later that year at her home in Switzerland.

4

With Margaret Gardiner and a dozen others at The Creel, St Margaret's Hope, enjoying a lobster supper as guests of a promising oligarch:

Oligarch: 'Margaret my dear, I fear I have come without my cheque book.'

5

25 June 2019. The world's best known living novelist Margaret Atwood, aboard a Canadian cruise ship somewhere in the Outer Hebrides, addresses Tom Muir, Orcadian storyteller and cruise lecturer:

'Tom, I'm so enjoying your book.'
Tom Muir: 'Er... em... er... isn't that my line?'
Atwood: 'All that fuss about cannibalism on the Franklin expedition. We've been gobbling one another up for centuries. Gobble, gobble, gobble!'
Muir: 'Like a field full of turkeys. Gobble, gobble, gobble!'

Exit Atwood, gobbling.

6

Beside a cruise ship, Kirkwall Pier:

Tour guide: 'Follow me please. Your bus is at the head of the pier, just 100 yards away.'

Cruise passenger: 'I'm from Milwaukee, and we don't walk!'

***

In the Wool Shop, Broad Street, Kirkwall:

'Can anyone tell me where I am? All I know is that we sailed from Belfast and called along Stornoway. But where am I now?'

***

Cruise passenger departing Kirkwall:

'I've really enjoyed Shetland. We are off now to Orkney!'

7

27 June 2019. At Gearrannan, a restored coastal blackhouse village in Lewis, Outer Hebrides:

'We used to grow all our own vegetables, but now Tesco delivers.'

8

28 June 2019. The 2019 joint Booker Prize winner, Margaret Atwood, comes upon Stromness Books and Prints:

CLOSED

9

Ithaca, USA: Cousin Elizabeth Ritch with her husband Professor Gary Okihiro of Cornell University attends a select dinner party. Her ears prick up when a greying curly-haired academic[2] mentions 'Orkney'. After explaining to the geographically and historically unlettered what and where Orkney is, he says:

'My mother had a house there, and what's more she has just given it away to a man who already has three!'
'And what's more,' pipes up Elizabeth, 'he is my cousin!'

10

Stromness, October 2017. I acquaint the Duke of Gloucester with the story of Alexander Graham:

'...and this fountain was erected so that horses might drink to his memory.'
'Do I detect humour?'

11

Shetland Airport, a white stretch limo at the taxi rank:

'Is this for me?'
'Only if you are Billy Connolly.'

12

Apologies to 'Hutch'.
David Hutchison ('Hutch'), clock doctor of Rackwick, carries a clock home in his wheelbarrow, and encounters an American tourist:

'Why are you carrying a clock in a wheelbarrow?'
'Because I can't afford a watch!'

13

Marjorie Linklater, champion of Orkney history and culture

A stalwart and forthright Scots Nat, Marjorie Linklater 'weekends' at Balmoral with her husband the internationally celebrated Orkney novelist Eric Linklater. Assisting the Queen (as one does) in cutting picnic sandwiches, she makes an unwise remark. The Queen freezes, knife in the air: 'Would you unseat me?'

* * *

An Orcadian Odyssey

On the death of Eric, Marjorie comes back to live in Orkney, and soon establishes herself as a leading figure in promoting local history and culture. She is also noted for a ready wit, and a forthright manner of speech:

'I've given up sex for committees!'

***

A delighted Marjorie recounts a conversation:

'Hello Mrs Linklater, what weather!'
'Yes, it's just pissing down!'
'You should have seen his face!'

***

'It's quite a thrill using my OAP pass to visit my lover!'

***

Marjorie Linklater stands before a bulldozer about to demolish a sand dune of particular scientific importance. Enraged bulldozer driver:

'You are a bugger and a whore!'
'Make up your mind. I can't be both!'

---

1 Sir Eduardo Paolozzi, Queen's Sculptor in Ordinary for Scotland, born in Leith to an Italian family of ice cream vendors. Examples of his work in the Pier Arts Centre collection
2 Professor Martin Bernal, son of Margaret Gardiner

17

Four Poets for St Magnus

A summer night in Outertown!
The light holds up, the dram
goes down!
Seamus Heaney

Elizabeth and Grenville

Even though they dwell in a
Land
In which roses cluster by open casements, mild
Zephyrs
About the house their fragrance spreading, languorous
Bees from
Every bloom spilling, yet still
They hold to the bare hill,
Heading sea
& breaking wave,
Glint of sun on
Riven rock; and so
Each summer they
Never fail their
Vision. Far
Into the North they fare,
Leave the balmy clime to
Live on the bare hill, absorb the
Ever fitful wind and surging sea.

An Orcadian Odyssey

> Published in 1987
> on the occasion of the 850th
> anniversary of the founding of
> the Cathedral of St Magnus, Orkney
> by Elizabeth Graham Scarth at
> The Breckness Press
> Orkney
>
> Introduction © George Mackay Brown, 1987
> Poems © the contributors, 1987
> Drawings © Bryce Wilson, 1987
>
> 'The Zodiac in the Shape of a Crown'
> appears in print for the first time
> by gracious permission of
> Their Royal Highnesses
> The Prince and Princess of Wales
>
> Designed by Ron Costley
>
> Printed in England by
> The September Press
> Wellingborough, Northants
> *and*
> Smith Settle
> Otley, West Yorkshire
>
> This edition is limited to one hundred copies
> of which fifteen bearing the letters A–O
> are not for sale
> of the remaining eighty five copies
> numbered 1-85, numbers 1-5
> are individually bound
>
> This is copy
>
> **D**
>
> *George Mackay Brown*
> *Ted Hughes*
> *Seamus Heaney*
> *Christopher Fry*
> *Bryce Wilson*

Above: *Four Poets for St Magnus* signed by the contributors
Facing page: Book and slipcase

Four Poets for St Magnus

One evening at the Pier Arts Centre I was cornered by a vivacious and slightly scary lady. This was Elizabeth Gore-Langton, born Elizabeth Graham Scarth of Skaill, but soon to be Elizabeth, Countess Temple of Stowe. Elizabeth and Grenville Gore-Langton left Hampshire every summer for their cottage, Garth, high on the hill overlooking Hoy Sound and Bishop Graham's palace of Breckness. Elizabeth had a passion for poetry, and regularly hosted poets during the St Magnus Festival. She was planning a limited edition of poetry to raise funds for St Magnus Cathedral on its 850th anniversary; would I care to illustrate it?

The book she envisaged, *Four Poets for St Magnus*, would contain works by George Mackay Brown and others of her acquaintance: Ted Hughes, Seamus Heaney and Christopher Fry. After a couple of years, and under Elizabeth's eagle eye, in 1987 the book was launched:

An Orcadian Odyssey

A summer night in Outertown:
The light holds up, the dram
                    goes down!
                        Seamus Heaney
P.S. You were missed.

A summer afternoon at Garth:
A good lunch, a welcoming
                    hearth

PS Looking forward to see you
            in Orkney...
17/7/94   George Mackay Brown

with Fabriano Roma hand-made paper sides, the front board being printed with a drawing by Bryce Wilson, titled in gold on the spine, in a cloth covered slipcase bearing a drawing in a sunk panel at £250.00 each.

From her days on secretarial duties at various British consulates, Elizabeth had become multilingual. A visit to Garth was always one of drink-fuelled talk and hilarity.

Four Poets for St Magnus

'The Kirk and the Ship' by George Mackay Brown

Ted Hughes attempted to recite in English a poem by a well known Hungarian, which he couldn't quite remember. Elizabeth's step-son Robert remembers:

> After listening to the great sage bang on for a bit, Elizabeth fixed him with that scary formidable look of hers and quoted back the poem he could not quite remember... in fluent Hungarian. She said 'So much better in the original, don't you think?' You have never seen a Poet Laureate so utterly gobsmacked.[1]

Four Poets for St Magnus raised £10,000 towards the upkeep of St Magnus Cathedral.

Elizabeth, grand-daughter of the distinguished Orkney poet and naturalist Duncan John Robertson, was dismissive of her own attempts at poetry – but there was one poem of which she was quite proud. It appears here by kind permission of her family.

An Orcadian Odyssey

Seal Woman

It was William who noticed it first, and William
    Who turned his questioning face to mine,
        'There's a strange smell of the sea'.
But I was fresh from the warmth of the laundry
      And all I could smell was linen.
      'Nothing unusual in that,' I said,
'With a sack of mackerel back in the passage
      There's always the smell of the sea'.
  His look slipped sideways, he turned away,
     And that was the day we took stock.

Oatmeal and flour, three hundredweight each,
Of sugar the same, that the slack time coming
Should not find us lacking; the peat in the yard
       In the stacks neat as dominoes.
  Hook in the kitchen trembling with hams,
      And tea in the lead-lined chests.

Was it late in the night that I heard the horses
    Thrash through the grass in the garden?
The snapping of castanet trot on the cobbles
      O currite currite noctis equi!
They swung past the house, the window panes rattled,
I threw back the covers and stood at the window
And felt the tide rise, rise on the vapour of night.
      The smell of the sea was stronger.
  The door of the passage is open, I thought
        As I sank into sleep.

I was stiff when I surfaced, and patterned in bruises
Darker than purple, darker than that of Imperial Caesar
Whose clay stopped the wind. And down on the shore
      Where the sea gnawed the land,
        A rustle of skulls.

Four Poets for St Magnus

Floundering round in the kitchen I broke
Two cups and a plate, and the saucepan handle
Kept slipping around till it fell on the flagstone floor.
The cats were happy, supping the porridge.
The fish had been taken outside.
Clumsily stumbling through Tuesday,
I scrubbed out the passages, reeking of fish:
It clung to me, stayed with me, kept me surrounded;
I breathed in, contented, the smell of the sea.

And the seventh wave will carry you in
To the seven tears on the shore.
I carried the hay to the stable.
The horses were tranced, their sweet breath rising
Like smoke from a sacrifice.
One of them whinnied. I found a sound to respond.

In my skull it tolled like a bell long silent,
Came out of my mouth like a gong
Again and again. The horses shifted.
I buried my head in the hay.

And the smell of the sea grew stronger.

My back had twisted when tossing the hay.
The pain bent me over, I slid to the floor.
My hands were stiffening, palms were hardening,
Bruises were spreading; my pelt grew dark.
I inched my way over and out through the door.

Heaving and dragging my way through the marshland,
My breathing heavy, I leaned to the wind.
And I drank the first
Thirst of the child at the breast,
The fresh, the cold, the familiar smell of the sea.

An Orcadian Odyssey

'I will be back!'

Recently, in Skaill House, a visitor saw a little girl skipping happily around the dining table, and took her photograph. Strangely, the child did not appear in the picture, nor was she any longer to be seen in the room. Explaining her experience to a member of staff, the visitor, suddenly noticing in the display a drawing of a child, exclaimed: 'And that is her!' – Elizabeth Graham Scarth of Skaill.

A few days after hearing of this incident I came upon the last Christmas card that I received from Elizabeth. There in frail hand was this firm declaration: 'I will be back!'

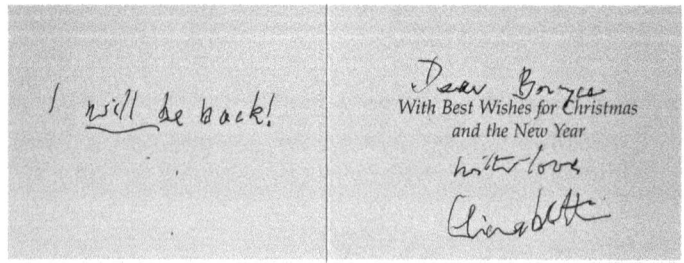

1 Quote from the Obituary by The Hon. Robert Chandos Temple-Gore-Langton, Orkney Heritage Society Newsletter, 2019

18

The Past in the Present

Stromness in the Orkney Islands is a town shaped by the sea. Built around a natural harbour, the houses reach out into the water, on a host of small piers and jetties washed by the tide. Here, the sea has borne the ships of many nations, and woven the life of the town into the great events of maritime history... The descendants of the great sea captains live in the houses they built, the stories of ocean adventure continue to inspire a spirit of energy and enterprise and community action amongst the people of the town.[1]

Sea Haven: Stromness in the Orkney Islands

There appeared one day at the Graemsay manse a young man with a camera, clearly suffering the effects of a stormy sea crossing. Born and raised in the mining town

An Orcadian Odyssey

Keith Hobbs

of Ashington in Northumberland where his father was GP, in his early years Keith Hobbs was drawn to ruined castles and coastal scenery. Trained in photography, he went freelance under his mother's Scots surname of 'Allardyce'. Drawn north to Orkney he had served as an RSPB warden, and a roving lighthouse keeper.

Over a restorative cup of tea, Keith Allardyce explained that he had been in touch with Howie Firth over an idea for a photographic record of Stromness, its history and current inhabitants. Would I provide the accompanying text? The chairman of the Stromness Community Council, Doris Stout, became deeply involved:

The Past in the Present

In 1989 the Stromness Community Council agreed to give financial support to the compilation of a photographic archive done over one year by Keith Allardyce, in collaboration with Orkney's Museums Officer, Bryce Wilson. The theme of the project – 'The past in the present' – aimed to show how the social and commercial aspects of present-day Stromness are intricately intertwined with the past. The buildings from a bygone era are not museum pieces – they are lived in and worked in by Stromnessians of today. The photographs provide continuity from the past into the present, and ahead to the future in enabling the next generation of Stromnessians to retain the links with the past that inevitably are fading in the present time of change... On behalf of the Community Council I sincerely wish to thank all the businesses and individuals, from Stromness and outwith, whose generous response and enthusiasm has allowed this project to reach fruition.[1]

Sea Haven: Stromness in the Orkney Islands was published in 1992 by the Orkney Press for Stromness Community Council. George Mackay Brown wrote:

It is a fine collection of photographs, and the accompanying text is deeply interesting and well written... I feel sure that some day a full detailed history of Stromness will be written.

An Orcadian Odyssey

A book to treasure and keep

Keith Allardyce returned to his native Northumbria. His work as an RSPB summer warden and later as a roving lighthouse keeper had deepened his affection for Orkney. A contract with the Northern Lighthouse Board brought him to produce *At Scotland's Edge*. This portrait of the last lightkeepers and their families, accompanied by their stories, became a valuable addition to the social history of Orkney, and Scotland in general.

A couple of decades later, with many books under his belt, he was back on my doorstep with a new idea. 'What about a book on beach combing? How would this go down – the found object and the story behind it?' The first edition of *Found*, published by The Orcadian Ltd, was a sell-out, and another was in the pipe-line.

Among the hundred or so beachcombers that Keith visited was Chris Rowell near Mill Bay in Hoy:

> The signs of a dedicated beachcomber lie all around the garden. Sea finds festoon every bush, path side, every ledge, everywhere. Radio 3 plays Mahler from an outside loud-speaker. Seal skulls, buoys and driftwood, large handles from army tea cups and mugs, plastic dolls, shells...

In the Foreword Tom Muir comments:

> He is a creative and original thinker...With the eye of an artist he brings out the best in the subject... whether it is a piece of flotsam washed ashore on an Orkney beach or the person who found it... This is a book to treasure and keep...

No candles flicker in the Hall of Clestrain;
Geramount in Sanday stands surreal and roofless;
ghosts stamp and twirl to fiddle and 'cello, in the
deserted ballroom of Scar.[2]

In the first volume of *Silent*, a portrait of deserted Orkney buildings, published in the year 2016, Keith remarks:

> The melancholy beauty of so many of the abandoned buildings across the Orkney landscape have long fascinated me... As an RSPB summer warden I stayed in the abandoned farmhouses of Copinsay and Swona. The poignancy of seeing the remnants of earlier endeavours to make a living in such apparently difficult circumstances has never left me...

The making of *Silent* included a scary expedition to Copinsay. Tom Muir describes it:

> Landing at the lighthouse pier we find that the structure has seen better days. Some of the railway sleepers that once formed it are no more and you are forced to jump over the gaps onto green slippery seaweed.[3]

In *Silent II* Keith has this to say:

> Special thanks go to my old friend Tom Muir for researching and writing around one hundred stories to enhance the photographs... He's achieved this during his busy life as Engagements and Exhibitions Officer at the Orkney Museum, and as a writer, broadcaster and international story teller. He completed work on the second volume of *Silent* just before embarking on a journey through Canada's North-West Passage, and over to Victoria Island,

An Orcadian Odyssey

Baffin Island and Greenland. On board a vessel of 'One Ocean Expeditions', he was invited to give lectures about Orkney pre-history and Orkney's celebrated explorer John Rae and the Hudson's Bay Company. No doubt a few Orkney folk tales were told along the way.

Keith also paid tribute to his partner: 'Finally, my thanks go to Ikuko Tsuchiya for all her support and love during our elegiac journey across Orkney.'

Among Tom's tales in *Silent II* is one of a visit to Graemsay:

> The ancient farmstead of the Netherhoose had a unique feature. It was well exposed to the prevailing westerly winds, and powerful gusts from Burra Sound and the neighbouring hills of Hoy. To counter this the occupants constructed the flag roofed close or passage that linked dwelling with byre and turnip shed, then wound its way up the brae to the barn with its grain drying kiln. Thus there was no need to go outside in rough weather. A large vertebra, from the whale that beached on Graemsay on 14th July 1906, was used at the Netherhoose as a milking stool.

At the end of the *Silent* project, Keith announced a group photograph:

> On the appointed day, armed with suitable props we all boarded Keith's sturdy vehicle, and off we set over the brae through Innertoon and Ootertoon, in search of a convenient ruin. Having successfully diverted Keith from the challenge of bumpy farm tracks, electric fences and fields of sharn and coos, we at last emerged unscathed at the foot of the Black Craig, and the remains of the long deserted

The Past in the Present

Rhonda Muir, Tom Muir, Keith Allardyce, Bryce Wilson, Ikuko Tsuchiya

croft of Craigside. 'Tom, will you please hold your telescope parallel to Rhonda's staff. That's better. And Iku, just move a little to the left. That's enough! Back a wee bit! Bryce, try and keep your eyes open.' Keith took his appointed place, and the camera clicked. 'That's it, folks.' Well, almost. Many clicks later, it was in the bag.[4]

Keith's untimely death early in 2018 was a sad loss to his partner Ikuko Tsuchiya and his many friends in Orkney and beyond. A seat has been placed in Keith's memory at Login's Well in Stromness.

1 *From Sea Haven: Stromness in the Orkney Islands* by Keith Allardyce 1992
2/3 From *Silent*, a portrait of deserted Orkney buildings by Keith Allardyce 2016
4 From *Silent II*, a further portrait of deserted Orkney Buildings by Keith Allardyce 2017

19

The Mermaid Bride

A year or so after the publication of *Sea Haven*, over a dram one evening Tom Muir declared that ideally all the Orkney folk tales should be brought together to make them available to new generations. I took a week's holiday at Swartafiold and produced a drawing of the Broonie of Copinsay. Tom took the hint. Five years and many tales and drams later, *The Mermaid Bride and other Orkney folk tales* was published and printed in 1998 by The Orcadian Ltd. The book sold out, and in a succession of reprints over two decades it is still an Orkney best-seller.

The Mermaid Bride

In the year 2003 Tom received a letter from Professor Yoshio Higashiura:

Some half a century ago, I had an opportunity of studying English linguistics and literature at  the University of Edinburgh on status of British Council scholar, 1953–54. After several Scottish tours in later years, I paid a visit to Orkney, and happened to find 'Mermaid Bride' at one of the bookshops on the main street of Kirkwall. I have been attracted by your 'gem-de-lovely' like tales as well as Mr. Bryce Wilson's fantastic illustrations. Now I am using 'Mermaid Bride' as a textbook in my English class, one of the activities of the Japan-Scotland Society, which led to Yamada's scheme for publishing the Japanese version of yours. Having just finished the whole work of translation, I am looking forward to having the first proof.

We firmly believe that the prospective Japanese edition will surely induce Japanese readers, young and old, to step into the legendary world nourished by imaginative islanders of Orkney who lived and are living on the opposite side of the globe, and fill them with amusement, wonder, and admiration.

The Japanese edition of *Mermaid Bride* was published by Alba Shobo in 2004. Several years later Dr Shimokusu Masaya of Doshisha University in Kyoto, having attended

An Orcadian Odyssey

Hoy's dark and lofty isle

a conference in Glasgow, brought his family to Orkney to get their copy signed. (My vision of a distinguished and greying academic was trumped by a young man wearing a t-shirt inscribed 'I belong tae Glesca'!) A party of the Japan-Scotland Society in 2019 explored Orkney and had their copies signed by author and illustrator. The Icelandic edition, translated by Jónu G Torfadóttur, was published in 2014 by Saemundur Press.

20
Cath & Karin

I hope this helps your Orcadian ancestors to swim with your Kai Tahu ancestors. We'll celebrate together in Orkney and Okarito!
Dedication in Cath Dunsford's novel *Song of the Selkies* for
Keri Hulme, Booker Prize winner, *The Bone People*

Among those who have contributed to the dissemination of Orkney culture and folklore are the Maori writer and publisher Dr Cath Dunsford and her partner, the German academic and translator Dr Karin Meissenberg. Cath Dunsford's novels *Song of the Selkies* and *Return of the Selkies* feature a group of shape-shifting storytellers of Inuit, Maori and Orcadian culture, confronting in Orkney the dark realities of the modern world. Speaking at a conference in Queen's University, Canada, the irrepressible Dunsford (who famously performed the Hakka in an international airport) refers to participation

An Orcadian Odyssey

Pacific Waiata to Viking Boat Burial, Scar, Sanday Orkney Islands
Cath Koa Dunsford '08

in the 14th Orkney International Science Festival:

> When Howie Firth asked us to take part in the 14th Orkney International Science Festival ... to do lectures in ecology and writing/publishing respectively, I was a bit sceptical ... But at this unique festival, science, art, music and practical workshops are blended with high academic papers given at the opening conference and somehow it all works out and has the public scrambling for seats and the halls packed out.

The highlight ... has been the visit of 25 Cree Nation men and women who are descended from Orcadian as well as Cree ancestry ... at the opening of the festival, the atmosphere at the packed Pickaquoy Centre was electric ... we danced hand in hand with the Cree until late into the night, our bodies electrified by their drumming and singing ... surrounded by painted faces and bright feathers and wings, Cree and Orcadian hand in hand ... It was very moving and humbling ... I felt very deeply honoured ...

'How do you teach science at First Nations University, Saskatchewan?' a scientist at the Orkney International Science Festival asks Cree Indian Professor Willie Ermine. Willie leans back, rubs his chin and thinks a while. Then he replies:

'We take the students fishing. We show them how to bait a line, throw it out, catch a fish, then we show them how to skin, fillet, salt, dry or smoke the fish and by the end of that process, we have covered a lot of scientific principles. Because they have taken part in the process, they will not easily forget it.'

Kia ora! 'Now that's the best definition of science I have ever heard,' I whisper to Karin.

'Cath & Karin' invited author and illustrator of *Mermaid Bride* to 'weekend' in Sanday:

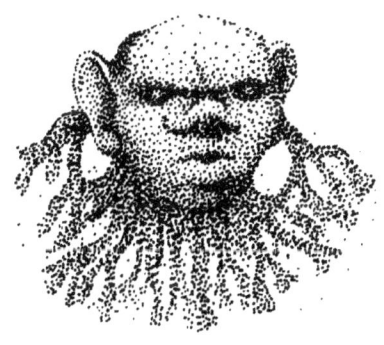

Cath & Karin

Claws full & succulent, the lobsters we
Ate by Sanday's Peerie Sea;
The new tatties from Neigarth
Had flavour sweet
& wholesome.
Keen-eyed
As gannets, we
Roamed the
Island shores, finding even a mermaid's purse – but
No sight or sound of the great selkie choir.

Maori symbols by Cath Dunsford

21

Babette

We walked the beaches and
were attracted by round stones
            perfectly round stones.
We were proud of round clay pots in our homes.
We admired round discs, the moon,
            when perfectly round.
    Our hands loved round things
    our eyes adored roundness
    in dancing our beings rejoiced in roundness.

In Praise of Perfect Roundness by Babette Barthelmess,
from *The Stone Ball from Towie, a Creation Hymn*, 2008

As a child, German-born Babette Barthelmess played amid the ruins of Berlin; she lost her father to the Second World War. She would go on to work as lecturer and researcher in Genetics and Molecular Biology at the

University of Hannover. It was while she chose to work at Edinburgh University between 1965 and 1971 that she discovered Orkney, and decided that this was where she wanted to live. She purchased the derelict holding of Duttentown in South Ronaldsay, spent much time and energy in restoring the property, and for many years it was her holiday home.

At last, in 1997, Babette came to live in Orkney. Over the next decade her wide interests would bring her down many paths, chiefly art and archaeology. 'I studied part-time Art and Design at Orkney College. Thereafter I hardly ever missed a chance to attend Anne Marie Nicol's evening classes in lino printing.'

Babette's house of Duttentown stood close to the Tomb of the Eagles in the parish of Burwick in South Ronaldsay. Here she witnessed the discovery of the tomb by Ronald Simison and her interest in archaeology was born. She wrote:

> From an eagle's perspective the Tomb of the Eagles can be spotted at the far southeast corner of South Ronaldsay securely perched above high cliffs. The taste of brine and the surge of the sea below are a reassuring presence. The entrance into the cairn faces away from the surrounding land towards the expanse of the North Sea in the east. It overlooks a natural amphitheatre formed by barren flagstones that slope gradually towards the sharp edge of the cliffs which drop a sheer 20–30m into the sea.
>
> Here, where wind, water and rock meet in a fierce embrace, Neolithic people created a sacred place to rest the bones of their ancestors. Was it more than just a tomb: a temple to worship the eternal cycles of life and death, light and dark, song and silence? ...In January 2001 I decided to experience the sunrise at the Tomb of the Eagles. Would the sun's rays ever reach into its dark womb?

Shaman, Babette Barthelmess

Over the next four years Babette arose early, sometimes very early, and armed with cameras and notebook set out for the tomb, often to be thwarted by cloud and fog. She at last made this discovery. On sunny mornings in early May and mid-August the whole length of the passage area is lit up from about 5.00 to 6.30 am.

> ...an alignment of the rising sun with the passage occurs not only in the spring but also in mid August.

Each year, around the autumn alignment, I found a noisy crowd of seals assembled on the steps of the pyramid-shaped rocks below the cliffs in front of the cairn. On sunny mornings from inside the tomb I heard them singing, bubbling, snorting, howling, and an air of great enchantment pervaded the place.

In 2004 there appeared the book *A Celebration of Sunrise at the Tomb of the Eagles* by Ilse Babette Barthelmess, a unique blend of art and science designed by the author, published by Orkney Museums and Heritage and printed by *The Orcadian*.

Babette Barthelmess

Before daybreak
And in all seasons,
Bearing cameras and compass, pen and paper,
    she makes for the
Entrance of the tomb, records
The sun's rising from the sea's rim, its golden path
To the tomb's door,
Enters then, dreaming, a world past minding.

Before her, the
Antlered shaman dances,
Ritually expressing
The sun's enduring,
Healing power.
Enchantment reigns. Selkies from the shore below
Lay their skins before the tomb and dance in
    human form.
Mythic birds remove the souls of the dead (bones of
Eagles in the tomb,
Skulls and ritual of broken pots).
She awakens to the selkies' song, far below in
    sea-washed caves.

Babette's fascination with the Neolithic was inflamed when she discovered the mysterious carved stone ball from Towie in Aberdeenshire in the National Museum of Scotland in Edinburgh. She wrote:

> The Ball of Towie is the most beautiful of well over 300 similarly sized stone balls found mostly in Aberdeenshire. In 2004 Joyce Gray from the Orkney Museum gave me the chance to investigate replicas of some of the 15 balls found in Orkney and to create clay replicas and even a piece of silver jewellery based on the symbols which I discovered on one of them – thanks to David Hodge's design and craftsmanship.
>
> Believing that the messages on the balls were not easily accessible to the average Neolithic contemporary I suggested the shaman as the likely spiritual interpreter and guardian of sacred knowledge in such societies.

Her studies of the Ball of Towie led her to suggest that the carved symbols on this ball represented a creation myth. In order to closely examine the ball, she created many artworks and twelve replicas from clay and stone. She communicated her findings as a poem *The Stone Ball from Towie, a Creation Hymn*, read and illustrated in a ten minute film on an attached DVD. It was part of a major exhibition of Babette's artistic work, 'COMPASSIONATE JOURNEYS – CONNECTING WITH OUR PAST', which opened in the Orkney Museum in March 2008.

Babette Barthelmess returned in 2006 to live in Hannover, but still spends part of every summer in Orkney, until the time when she hopes to rest at the Flaws Cemetery, South Ronaldsay, next to her former friends and neighbours.

22

Back at the Ranch

Meanwhile, 'back at the ranch', more display space was required to accommodate growing collections. Stromness Museum was overflowing, but the tenancy of the adjoining private house had been relinquished. The owner had disappeared in America a century before, and the property had fallen to the Crown Estate. After discussion with Orkney Islands Council an approach was made. The Crown responded favourably. Ownership would be transferred to the Orkney Islands Council, on condition that they restored the building and handed it over to the Museum. The Council accepted, and this generous gesture led to four additional galleries: Deep Sea Shipping, Coastal Traders, Arctic Whaling and the

Sea Captain's Parlour. Space was now released in the main building for expanded displays on Stromness, the Fishing Industry, the Lighthouses of Orkney, The Scuttled German Fleet, the Hudson's Bay Company and its Arctic explorer, Dr John Rae. The additional building, named 'The Pilot's House' for the sea pilot who built it, was opened in 1996.

A professional survey of the main building was prompted by the precarious state of the 130-year-old roof. This revealed that the weight of half a ton of fossils, not to mention a number of heavy storage heaters, was putting an excessive strain on the upper floor: access to the Natural History galleries could no longer exceed a dozen visitors. A public appeal brought in cash for the replacement of the roof. The Natural History galleries of the first floor had been closed, and the only solution to strengthening the floor would be the insertion of steel beams. In the process the whole building would be stripped and replastered, rewired, and an oil powered heating system inserted, along with burglar and fire alarm. The visitor experience would be improved with toilet and disabled access, new lighting and display cases.

The onerous task of raising the major funding from local and national sources, and the Hudson's Bay Company in Canada, fell to the Honorary Secretary Jim Troup and the Treasurer, Ron Leonard, to raise the necessary half million pounds. At the same time, the Museums Service took on the lengthy task of cataloguing and packing the exhibits for storage in the former Orphir School. One of the archaeological artefacts was recorded as 'Fragment of whale bone with bored holes, Skarabrae'. Much later it was recognised by Dr David Clarke of the National Museum as the first Stone Age figurine to have been discovered in Scotland.

Jim Troup, Honorary Secretary of Stromness Museum, sent this appeal in 1998 to the Rupert's Land *Newsletter of the University of Winnipeg*:

An Orcadian Odyssey

Do you remember Stromness Museum? The walk along the narrow main street, twisting and turning, rising and falling, with ever and anon a glimpse of the sea between the sturdy stone houses? A walk that was a pleasant feature of the 1990 Colloquium. That conference was immensely enjoyed by everyone in Orkney who had any connection with it.

At the end of the guided walk the museum – a venerable institution (founded in 1837) within a dignified Victorian building of 1858 close by the shore – rich in maritime and natural history displays, and above all for Canadians, rich on its HBC connection. Since then the 'Nor West' display has been strengthened. The John Rae Centenary exhibition, *No Ordinary Journey,* was unfortunately seen only in Edinburgh and in Kirkwall [the proposed showing in Canada proving impractical]. When it was dispersed Stromness Museum was offered all that had been specifically made for that exhibition including Rae himself seated in a Halkett air-boat, paddling with tin dinner plates across an Arctic river. Appropriately the only survivor of those early inflatables is just a few feet away.

Expansion into the neighbouring house gave Bryce Wilson the opportunity to improve greatly the display of ship models, whaling and Inuit relics and led on to honours with the award of a special prize in the 1996 H. E. Scottish Museum of the Year competition.

If you should be in Orkney, do come and enjoy an hour. But not this winter. The Museum has just closed for a major renovation and upgrading that will take six or seven months. By the end of May the ground floor and Pilot's House extension will be re-opened and for the year 2001 the whole building in all its glory. This is at immense cost (over half a million Canadian dollars). Most of the funding is in place but

Back at the Ranch

there is still a sizeable shortfall. Any contributions would be gratefully received.

After eighteen months of reconstruction, the museum was back in shape, and reopened with fanfare and rejoicing. Care had been taken to preserve the character of the building, including the extensive Victorian collections of taxidermy that had, in the 'politically correct' fashion of the times, been abandoned by most other museums throughout the country. A painting of the last Great Auk

From the ethnographic collection, Stromness Museum

of Papa Westray, funded by the Governor of the Hudson's Bay Company David E Mitchell, and the Museums and Galleries Purchase Fund, marks the achievements of Jim Troup and Ron Leonard who by sheer hard work had made the reconstruction financially achievable.

23

A Pivotal Role

However the 'merchant lairds' of Orkney may have regarded themselves, they owed their very existence, and a duty of care, to the tenantry that tilled their fields, fished their waters and laboured on their kelp shores to bolster their comfort and self-esteem. As time went on trade became the province of a rising merchant class, distancing the landed families even farther from their roots to seek wealth and political advantage abroad. The cathedral of Saint Magnus, the palaces of earl and bishop and the substantial town houses that grace the winding street of the Royal Burgh of Kirkwall stand as a memorial for many generations of artists, tradesmen and labourers.

A century ago, the age-old structure of laird and tenant collapsed before the advance of the 'peerie laird', regaining ownership and independence after centuries of subsistence farming and cap doffing. With a nod to the Baikie family, the elegant rooms of Tankerness House now have a pivotal role in telling the Orkney story in all its variety, over more than 5,000 years.

An Orcadian Odyssey

Orkney Museum

The formation of a museum to display the stored collections of the Orkney Antiquarian Society had long been discussed. Thanks to the efforts of the County Librarian Evan MacGillivray, the painter Stanley Cursiter, the Provost of Kirkwall James Flett and others, Tankerness House would be restored to house both a museum and the offices of the royal burgh. With grants from the Pilgrim Trust and the Historic Buildings Council for Scotland, the restoration was carried out by Ian G Lindsay and Partners of Edinburgh, winning a Civic Trust award.

The Council followed professional advice that the whole building be turned into a museum. A team of students from the Museum Studies Department of Leicester University worked with the newly appointed Honorary Curator Evan MacGillivray, who now occupied a spacious flat overlooking the gardens. Tankerness House Museum was opened by R B K Stevenson, Keeper of the National Museum of Antiquities of Scotland, on Friday 31st May, 1968.

24
Retelling the Orkney Story

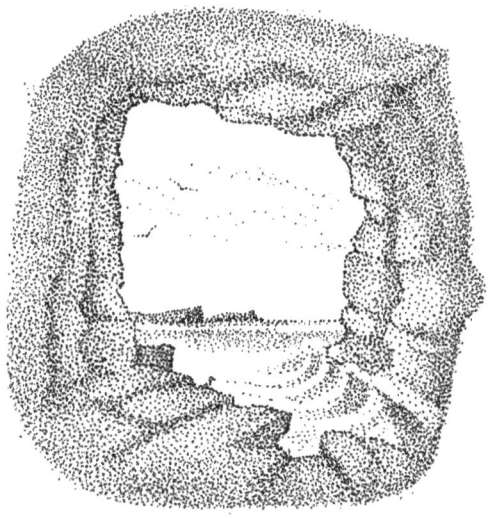

I have spent most of my working life interpreting the story of Orkney through museum displays; not, I may say, purely for the growing tourist industry, but primarily for the resident population, and particularly for the young. Much of the background information came from archive material and rare books, all available for study in the Orkney Library; and from fine histories produced during the 19th and early 20th centuries by visiting and resident authors. They were all rather expensive, and for most Orkney folk buying books was well beyond their priorities. Then there came a man intent on filling the gap.

An Orcadian Odyssey

...and be read by every Orkney boy and girl before their schooldays are over

As a schoolboy John Gunn had walked barefoot from the farm of Howe, with a peat under his arm, to the Parish School in Stromness. He went on to university and eventually became editor-in-chief for the Edinburgh publishers Thomas Nelson and Sons. From this elevated position, in 1909 he published *The Orkney Book, Readings for Young Orcadians*:

> *This is a book about Orkney, for use in Orkney, designed and for the most part written by natives of Orkney. It owes its origin to the Edinburgh University Orcadian Association, the members of which realized the desirability of preparing a general view of their homeland ... suitable to all, in the hope that the book may find its way into every school in the county, and be read by every Orkney boy and girl before their schooldays are over.*

With cover design and other decorative features by a young student at Edinburgh College of Art, Stanley Cursiter, The Orkney Book found a place in Orkney schools and libraries, and a smattering of private bookshelves. It was followed a couple of decades later by Gunn's *ORKNEY, The Magnetic North*. Aimed at encouraging and informing visitors from 'the adjacent island' of Great Britain, it was affordable and popular enough to run to ten editions, and it was welcomed in many otherwise book-free Orkney homes. The New Orkney Book, with Stanley Cursiter still involved, along with many local writers, was published by Nelson in 1966 to be distributed to all Orkney schools.

William Clairkis house now bigged

Not long after his appointment as Head of History at Stromness Academy, James Troup was engaged to write a short history of Stromness, in celebration of the 150th anniversary of the Burgh. His professional expertise brought him to the Orkney Library & Archive in Kirkwall. Here among the sasine records he discovered a feu charter in which Earl Robert Stewart granted William

Clark and his wife Mareon Chalmer the right to open an inn by the eastern shore of Hamnavoe. There followed a note in the 1595 Bishopric Rental: 'William Clairkis house now bigged'.

Further probing in the archives revealed feus of bishopric land, responding to the rapid growth of Atlantic shipping:

> Chalmer's Quoy ... an area of some 240 feet square' when presented in 1624 to Alexander Chalmer, a smith, and his wife, Janet Firth, was 'waist ground on the west ryd of his raid [the Bishop's bay or roadstead] of Cairston'; all for an annual feu of 24 chickens.

The result of Jim Troup's researches, *Stromness, 150 Years a Burgh 1817–1967*, included a comprehensive geographical survey 'The Town in its Setting' by the geography teacher Frank Eunson. It was well illustrated by photographs from the Museum collection, and fine pen drawings by a senior pupil, Sandy Young. On this framework George Mackay Brown wove *The Pageant of Stromness* that enthralled full houses in Stromness Town Hall during the anniversary celebrations.

In 2002, as a parting gesture I was asked to tell the story of the Baikie family, whose town house had been my place of work for nigh on thirty years. Kirkwall Grammar School's Rector Willie Thomson referred me to his colleague the historian Ray Fereday to examine the draft of *Profit Not Loss, the Story of the Baikies of Tankerness*. Ray responded with ten closely typed pages:

> When you have pondered over these remarks and the informed advice of Willie Thomson and Sheena Wenham you can make a few changes, not many will be needed. Have you had a chat with Thora Bain? Despite her age she had her wits about her

Retelling the Orkney Story

when I met her last summer, and if she could glance through I am sure that she could contribute an anecdote or two. Presumably she is still at Lyness Cottage, Junction Road. Once she is warmed up she will go on in fine fashion.

Ray Fereday's many enlightened comments ensured a much better book, published by Orkney Heritage in 2003.

The Ring of Brodgar

25

Two Distinguished Historians

Over the latter decades of the 20th century the presentation of Orkney history benefited hugely from the presence of two distinguished historians – William P L Thomson, Rector of Kirkwall Grammar School, and his colleague and friend, Dr Ray P Fereday, Principal Teacher of History. Between them they challenged J Storer Clouston's assertion that after the fall of the Stewart earls and the abolition of Norse Law 'the history of the "country of Orkney" ends, and the annals of a remote Scottish county begin.'

William PL Thomson OBE
Photo © Rebecca Marr

Willie Thomson, born in Ayrshire, was Principal Teacher of History and Geography in Shetland's Anderson Institute, and became Assistant Headmaster. He was in 1971 appointed Rector of Kirkwall Grammar School. During his thirteen years in Shetland he had also been vice-chair of the Shetland Labour Party, but declared that 'he found Orcadians less argumentative than the Shetlanders, and he preferred that'.[1]

From Papdale House,

originally the home of Malcolm Laing, author of a celebrated *History of Scotland*, Thomson gave up political activity to examine the many aspects of Orkney's past.

Of his *History of Orkney*, first published in 1987, his obituarist the Shetland archivist Brian Smith declared that there was 'no history of a Scottish county to match it'. His volume *The Little General and the Rousay Crofters* (1981) examined the life and notoriety of one of Orkney's last major landowners.

Over some thirty years he produced half-a-dozen seminal books and many papers and articles, in particular on the kelp industry, Orkney farm names, crofting and agricultural change, and the dissolution of Orkney's farming estates. He was awarded OBE for a major contribution to the study of Scottish history.

It reads like a soap opera

Willie Thomson's comrade-at-arms, Ray Fereday from Birmingham, spent seventeen years as Principal Teacher of History at Kirkwall Grammar School. His friendship with Ernest Marwick, along with a robust constitution, led to his exploration of the islands through walking and coastal sailing, and spurred his interest in Orkney's past. Willie Thomson commented:

> The half-hour before the beginning of the school-day is usually a busy time, requiring all sorts of last-minute arrangements. But if, as was often the case, Ray had been in the archives on the previous evening, all thoughts of immediate problems were put out of our minds... I do not think that our priorities were wrong.

Grist to Ray's mill were adventurous school outings, sometimes to explore the sea caves where Jacobite lairds hid from Hanoverian troops, and young islanders from naval

An Orcadian Odyssey

impressment. His PhD from Aberdeen University was obtained for a thesis on *The Lairds of Eighteenth Century Orkney*, and he has done more research than anyone else into the 50,000 documents of the Balfour papers preserved in the Orkney archives. From *Phin of Finstown* and *The Longhope Batteries and Towers* (1971), through *Orkney Feuds and the '45* (1980), he has contributed articles to *The Orcadian*, *Orkney Heritage* and *Orkney Studies*, as well as chapters to *The People of Orkney* (1980).

Ray Fereday

Retirement with his wife Jean to Plymouth meant regularly driving the length of Britain to visit their many friends and delve further into the Orkney archives. At last came *The Orkney Balfours 1747–99* (1990), a rollicking tale which in the writer's own words 'reads like a soap opera'. He returns to Orkney whenever he can. To mark his major contribution The Fereday Prize is awarded annually for local history projects by pupils at Kirkwall Grammar School and Stromness Academy.

1 Obituary by Brian Smith, Shetland Archives, *The Orcadian*, July 28, 2016

26
Bursting at the Seams

By the end of the 20th century the Orkney Museum was bursting at the seams. Stone Age, Bronze Age, Iron Age, Picts and Vikings now occupied the whole south wing of Tankerness House. Part of the property fronting onto Broad Street was let as a shop and a cafe with the curator's flat above. The leases were not renewed, and plans were approved to double the museum's display space. I would relinquish the curator's flat. Access from the Viking gallery would be gained through the adjoining wee room (where the Baikies had powdered their wigs!) and up a stair to the flat by demolishing part of the intervening stone gable.

The way was clear for another thousand years of Orkney history. The former flat accommodated the Medieval world, Scotification, the Stewart Earls and the Merchant Lairds. Down a stair in the former shops we placed Victorian Orkney, two World Wars and Modern Times. These last two galleries were opened at Easter 2003. With nowhere left to go, it seemed like a good time to shed the white gloves.

An Orcadian Odyssey

Footsteps on the stair!

Early in my career I was alone one day in Tankerness House at lunchtime with the doors locked. I heard footsteps on the upper floor. I mentioned this to the custodian John Windwick, who responded: 'So you've heard it, have you?' On another occasion I was startled by a loud stamping on the stair. One day when I was away a painter was alone in the museum at lunchtime. When John Windwick returned he said, 'Would Bryce have come in at dinner time? I heard footsteps on the stair.' Over time, all staff members experienced the footsteps. William Cowan, who lived there early in the 20th century, had spoken of 'strange sounds'.

Among the visitors to Tankerness House was Naomi Mitchison CBE. Referred to as the doyenne of Scottish novelists, she came from time to time to Orkney from her home in Carradale, Argyllshire, where she worked tirelessly to improve the prospects of the local fishing community. Staying in Kirkwall with her friend Marjorie Linklater, she spoke of the Bakgatla tribe in Botswana of which she had been adopted adviser and mother. Learning that she had suffered a hip injury, they got their heads together and practised voodoo: pain and injury disappeared.

Naomi Mitchison had a keen interest in the first settlers of Orkney, the neolithic farmers who created the great stone monuments that punctuate the landscape. This resulted in *Early in Orcadia*, in which she envisaged a family crossing the firth in a skin boat to settle on the island that is now known as South Ronaldsay. The author envisaged a pilgrimage to a great temple at the Ness of Brodgar, decades before it was revealed by an archaeological dig.

Naomi Mitchison to Margaret Gardiner:

'Do you remember? We met on the sleeper from London.'
'Yes, and I got no sleep for the clatter of your typewriter!'

27

A Tale of Boom and Bust

Stromness

Salt, the winds
That whip the piers,
Rattle the snecks, fling
Open the doors,
Moan in the eaves & sigh in the gardens. From
North &
East &
South they blow – but there's
Shelter from the west.

Stromness had come into its own when changes in international trade brought shipping from ports around the North Sea and the Baltic heading to and from the Atlantic. Stromness folk were accustomed to conversing with strangers. One of the diarists of the Stanley Expedition to Faroe and Iceland, whose ship the brig *John* dropped anchor in June 1789, observed:

> this being the best [inn] in Town... the Landlady Mrs Allan, she by way of Joking told us the Danes were entitled to the Reign of Government... she had been in Denmark & spoke that language... she had also been in the West Indies... had been living 9 years in St. Croix.

An Orcadian Odyssey

HBC Ships at Stromness, 1819, painted by Midshipman Robert Hood (Private Collection)

With the growth of steam shipping during the 19th century, fewer and fewer sailing vessels required a 'pit stop' in Stromness; the once flourishing building of wooden vessels decreased and petered out at the turn of the 20th century, as did the herring fishing that had brought wealth to the town. On the other hand, regular steam powered cargo vessels had opened Orkney's door to a farming revolution. Stromness now became a prosperous market for the greatly increased export of sheep and cattle and other farm produce.

Following the 150th anniversary of the burgh in 1967, the economy of Stromness took a downward turn. While the winding street was now protected as a conservation area of national importance, most of the shops and businesses that had created it had disappeared into the all-consuming maw of the supermarkets and the internet. The generation that had endured the Depression and two World Wars now witnessed the draining of the town's trade. They would be astonished to learn that the sea once again brought the world to its door. The former Stromness Academy and Primary School now housed the Orkney campus of Heriot-Watt University, a world leader in the research of renewable energy, along with a maritime research hub of Robert Gordon University. Dozens of postgraduate students stream annually through their doors. Wave energy devices are tested in the turbulent tides of Hoy Sound, and Aquatera, employing more than thirty people, offers environmental expertise around the world. Over the centuries and into the future, the importance of incoming talent to the town, both culturally and economically, cannot be over-emphasised.

28

Will Your Anchor Hold?

God help any nation which neglects to study its past.
It is the very essence of our present and future ages.
Robbie Sutherland – Will Your Anchor Hold?

That ebullient Stromness seafarer Robbie Sutherland made his mark in Orkney when he developed the 'Sea School', Orkney Islands Council's response to unemployment among the farming community.

Robbie Sutherland and Inga Mal-Voy
Photo © Selena Kusman

Robbie's schoolmate, George Mackay Brown, celebrated his seventieth birthday:

> **CAPTAIN ROBBIE: 70**
> *27 August 1994*
>
> *Robert Sutherland, master mariner, famous Orkneyman*
> *Born in Hamnavoe; where else would an*
>   *Orkney sailor*
> *Embark on this*
> *Round watery globe, but from*
> *This town, daughter of the sea?*
>
> *So for a few years our sailor was*
> *Under the horizon,*
> *Trading world-wide, far from*
> *Hoy Sound and the Holms, making brief landfalls*
> *East and west.*
> *Restless they are, mariners, but they all*
> *Long for*
> *A last landfall, following the Psalmist's time-chart.*
> *Now welcome your wanderer,*
> *Daughter of the sea, Stromness, give him happy*
>   *anchorage.*
>
> GMB
>
> *A happy birthday, Robbie*
>   *from George.*

Having conquered alcoholism and endured a failed marriage, Robbie was reunited with his soulmate Inga Mal-Voy: 'The great good fortune of fate brought back into my life the great love I lost, as a consequence of my affliction.' At their hospitable seafront home, named *Dalhanna* after his second ship, Inga supported him in all matters of family and friends, teaching and business interests, and then in retirement, his writing and publication of several books, beginning with *Romiosini* [Seeking the unattainable] published in 1998. From the flyleaf:

> Robbie charts the highs and lows; his happiness and success at sea, and the horrible temptations in port, where he built up an eventual addiction to alcohol which threatened his career and his life… he overcame alcoholism… With sometimes devastating honesty, the author examines his life and influences and is not afraid to confront the darker side of himself. He also explores his great happiness – his love of sea-life, and his great enjoyment of women.
>
> Becoming a teacher, and settling to family life, he tackled his new career with characteristic enthusiasm, eventually returning to Orkney as Head of Department at the brand new Stromness Nautical School. Throughout his sometimes turbulent new career, Robbie spoke out against bureaucracy and, as he sees it, the wrong-headed decision-making which threatens the future of Orkney's sea-going life and traditions.

When Robbie inherited the care of a large collection of family letters, photographs, cuttings and documents, he set about recording the tale, published in 2002 under the title *Will Your Anchor Hold? The Story of an Orkney Seafaring Family 1850–2000*. The back cover states:

> This book re-examines some of the events and people, from the small and obscure to the well-known and global which helped shape not only the author but all of us… God help any nation which neglects to study its past. It is the very essence of our present and future ages.

29

'Cheust sometheen gaun aboot!'

Capiliera, in the foothills of the Sierra Nevada, Spain

If I got my finger out in retirement, I was told, I could in a couple of years have an exhibition of paintings and drawings in the Orkney Museum. Skills acquired at art school had chiefly been absorbed in museum display, and in book illustration. I now had a go at landscape and portraiture, some of which is included in this odyssey.

I had more time to travel. Other than a school trip to Paris I had never been abroad until in the late '70s, when my friend Alfie Taylor, pottery teacher at Kirkwall Grammar School, invited me to spend Easter with him at his home in Nerja on Spain's Costa Del Sol.

'Es bueno verte Alfredo!' [Good to see you Alfred!] In the narrow winding Calle el Barrio Alfie's neighbours were the farmers and fishermen and tradesmen who had outlived the civil war and the despotism of Franco. The aroma of freshly baked bread pervaded the early morning street. Alfie's house with its red-tiled roof had been little altered. In former times a donkey would have been stabled on the ground floor.

Next door in the shade sat old Tia, toothless and black attired, dispensing draughts of rough red wine from a big white jug; and beyond, on the strip of land by the sea a farmer turned the soil, his plough drawn by a pair of sturdy milking cows.

A few miles inland was the beautiful hill town of Almuñécar, now prospering on the tourist trail. When the young Laurie Lee stayed there in the '30s it was a place of dire poverty. The election of a socialist government raised wild hopes, soon to be dashed by civil war. Tourism had barely touched the foothills of the Sierra Nevada. High on the steeps of the Alpujarra farmers had for more than a thousand years tended spring-watered terraces, constructed by the Moors as 'the granary of Granada'. In Capiliera a goat was skinned, cooked over charcoal and served for our supper with lashings of country wine.

In Granada, in the water gardens of the Alhambra, palace of the Moorish kings, Japanese tourists confronted the morning frost with nose cosies. Full-throated young priests strummed guitars, weaving their Easter passion through the streets and bars of the city. In the evening at the Hotel Washington Irving, fur-clad women sat by the bar, sipping iced cocktails and breathing fog.

In Nerja on Good Friday the Calle el Barrio was decorated and strewn with palm fronds; carpets and bed covers hung from the balconies. In the evening the gilded Madonna emerged from the church shoulder high, processing around the town to the beat of drums, far into the night. A penitent dragged a great wooden cross.

'Cheust sometheen gaun aboot'

I think thoo're gaan tae Egypt!

At New Year 1998, Ruby Skinner examined my tea leaves: 'Thoo're aff on a lang journey… I think thoo're gaan tae Egypt!' I had told nobody. The previous year terrorists had massacred tourists at the temple of Hatshepsut, so the terms were favourable. Learning that I would visit the Valley of the Kings, Margaret Gardiner said: 'Mention my father's name.' When I dropped Sir Alan Gardiner's name our guide said: 'His was the first book I was required to read.'

While admiring the great temple of Abu Simbel I felt a tap on my shoulder: 'We hear you're from Orkney. Do you know Ingrid Tait?' In a carpet shop in Luxor, a turbaned and robed gentleman was seated cross-legged and smoking a hookah. He asked where I came from. 'Oh, you're from Scotland! My nephew has a shop in Aberdeen.'

Don't visit Thailand in May

In May 2003 I made a long planned visit to cousin Maurice and his family in Brunei. On the way I spent time in Bangkok. My inflight reading advised: 'Don't visit Thailand in May.' A sweat-drenched week revealed myriad Buddhist temples, glitteringly tiled and gilded. Marketeers clamoured on the teeming river, and tuk-tuks[1] ran pell-mell, dodging traffic on chaotic streets. Food was freshly cooked in street-side stalls, and the pavement was shared with wretched beggars.

Well fed and watered

A three-hour flight reached the oil-rich sultanate of Brunei, tucked away on the north eastern coast of Borneo. Maurice was architect of the sultan's new treasury, soon to be commissioned. Its 'dark and lofty' tower was based on a Scottish keep; we partied on the roof. Dropping anchor by a Pacific island we swam ashore to enjoy fishy delights. Well fed and watered we spent the night: a feast for bed bugs.

An Orcadian Odyssey

Mulu, Borneo May 03

My, you've come a long way!

From Brunei the tiny plane scrambled over the mountain tops and plunged into the world heritage site of Mulu, in the rain forest of Sumatra. Stilted dwellings lined the river banks and the villagers displayed their wares – exquisitely woven bags and baskets. In the dark of evening food was served in a roofed area open to the elements: a bat shot between spoon and mouth. This was the year of the Sars pandemic, so few folk had been brave or foolish enough to venture abroad:

'We are from Northern England. How about you?'
'I'm from Northern Scotland.'
'My, you've come a long way!'

Coasting homewards, the blinds were raised over a boundless sea of cloud, pierced only by the mighty Matterhorn. We had begun the descent to Heathrow.

'Cheust sometheen gaun aboot'

Thingvellir (Photo: Tom Muir)

Deus du get aroond muckle?

In June 2006 we set sail, Ola and Arnie Tait, Roberta Clubb and me, to tour Iceland in Arnie's 4x4. Also on the voyage were Tom Muir and Laurence Tulloch, to tell stories. From Seydisfyordur in the east we rode Iceland's southern highway through swathes of blue lupin and velvet moss. We ticked off the ancient glacier of Vatnajökull and the new-born island of Surtsey; the thundering falls of Gullfoss, and the spouting geyser. At Thingvellir, where the Earth's tectonic plates part company, Norse settlers first held the Althing, the oldest parliament in the world. North from Reykjavik lay Reykjaholt with its fertile farmlands. Here Snorri Sturluson[2] wrote the sagas, and languished in a thermal bath. Onwards to Lingabrekka: Tom and Laurence told tales, a Pet Viking[3] was born, and Steindór Andersen sang the songs of Iceland. Roberta to Andersen:

> 'Deus du get aroond muckle?'
> 'Well, I'm just back from performing in the New York Met, and I'm heading for the Barbican in London.'

We ploughed northwards over a vast sulfurous plateau, home of trolls and outlaws, descending to the lush pastures of the northern coast. Warmed by the unsetting sun we succumbed to the galleries and pavement cafés of Akureyri.

An Orcadian Odyssey

Eastward then to complete the circle of ice and fire: to Myvaten, the 'midgie' lake, created by a huge volcanic eruption, and the Godafoss falls, where the old Norse gods were tossed into the torrent to make way for Christianity.

A horse-drawn sleigh... drove right past me

In October 2010 we cruised from St Petersburg to Moscow through rivers and lakes and canals on 'the waterway of the Tsars'. There was much to enjoy and ponder over during our twelve day voyage. Against a daily diet of Russian icons, with magnificent bravura Cossacks leapt and sang, the Mariinsky Ballet pliéd and pirouetted, and scores of balalaikas evoked the steppes of Russia. Grim-faced women patrolled the Russian Museum. The Nouveau Riche paraded the galleries of GUM, while at street corners the poor and dispossessed exchanged matches and wild flowers for pennies.

At the Kizhi Open-Air Museum I drew the scene before me – a windmill, a clump of trees and a distant chapel. Years later while watching the film *Anna Karenina*, the same scene appeared, covered in snow; then a horse-drawn sleigh, carrying Anna and Count Vronsky, drove right past me. I waved.

'Cheust sometheen gaun aboot'

On the last day, for those of us who were not, as Arnie declared, totally 'iconed out', a visit was planned to the monastery of Sergiev Posad – posted as one of Russia's holiest places – some 60 miles by bus from Moscow. On the way we drove through ancient timber-built villages, now in decline as young folk headed for the attractions of city life. We passed army training camps, where the youth of Russia spend one year of national service. We saw a district crowded with tiny dachas on small plots of land. These Comrade Joseph Stalin, bless him, had given to the people of Moscow that they might cultivate and preserve summer fruits to leaven the snowbound winter.

At last the monastery came into sight, with its great white walls and domes of blue and gold. Our visit coincided with the anniversary of the founder, St Sergiev, who died some 600 years before. An open air mass was about to take place. We were surrounded and carried along to the monastery's central square by the hundreds who had gathered from Moscow and the communities around. We made way for the patriarch of the Russian Orthodox Church with a legion of bishops, all crowned and robed in green and gold. A deep, rich baritone led a great massed choir, punctuated by the clang and clatter of bells from the surrounding churches and chapels.

1. Tuk-tuk – three-wheeled motor-cycle taxi
2. Snorri Sturluson, 1179–1241. Historian, poet and politician, writer of Heimskringla, the sagas of the Scandinavian kings
3 Hjörleifur Helgi Stefánsson, of an old Icelandic farming family, came to Orkney to learn the storyteller's craft: 'It was not until I met my brother of lore, Tom Muir of Orkney, that I knew there was such a thing as a storyteller. He taught me what little I know about delivering a story; I proudly hold the title "Pet Viking"… without him it is quite possible that no one would sit through my ramblings or read my gibberish.' Hjörleifur cut his teeth before strangers in the author's home in Stromness and became a renowned storyteller, both in Iceland and abroad. His first book, *Icelandic Folk Tales*, was published in 2020 by The History Press.

30

Stromness: A History

'I feel sure that some day a full detailed history of Stromness will be written.'
George Mackay Brown

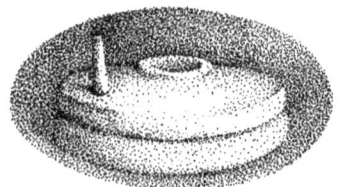

The 200th anniversary of the Burgh of Stromness was on the horizon. With the encouragement of Jim Troup, in 2009 I put away pencil and paintbrush and took on the task of producing 'a full detailed history of Stromness'. In the Museum stood a cabinet bursting with files on the history of the town. Ray Fereday now dug out from his copious card index every source of reference to Stromness, paving the way for many fruitful visits to the Orkney Library & Archive. He read every word of the first draft, making many useful comments and criticisms, as did that meticulous grammarian (and GMB's amanuensis) Maureen Gray, rounding up and penning a flock of straying punctuation marks.

After many revisions and additions, in September 2013 *Stromness: A History* was ready for the press. *The Orcadian* kindly published and printed a hardback edition of 2,000 copies, in good time for the 200th anniversary, in 2017, of the Burgh of Stromness.

What on earth could you find tae say aboot Graemsay?

I had for many years collected every scrap of information about Graemsay, land of my forebears, Stromness's nearest island neighbour and for centuries an unfailing contributor to the town's economy. With a tenfold reduction in its population there were now few to tell the tales. Graemsay is one of Orkney's smaller inhabited islands but, as they say, size is no indication of stature. The question 'What on earth could you find tae say aboot Graemsay?' was sufficient, and *Graemsay: A History* was published late in 2015. So that no newcomer need live in ignorance of its history, every habitable house of the island received a complementary copy.

A gathering of all the Orkney themes

There is a wealth of information on Orkney's history and prehistory, much of it scattered in specialist books and papers. The British Museum had published *A History of the World in 100 Objects*. In the modern world with its many distractions, would Orkney benefit from such a book, a gathering of all the Orkney themes, albeit briefly, under one cover? James Miller at The Orcadian Ltd agreed. As the book progressed it became apparent that the text mattered a trifle more than the illustrations, so we agreed on 'tales' rather than 'objects': for each tale a page of text, with an equal space for illustrations. Readers looking for more on any particular topic might then consult the book list attached. *Orkney in a Hundred and One Tales* came out in November 2018 in time for the Christmas market. Feedback indicated that many readers approved the format. One national reviewer wished that the stories were longer – I rest my case.

In Memoriam

Calfee Nicol
Girning Johnny
Laughin' Tammy
Soor Alice
Mealy Annie
Burstane Chrissy
Bella Pudeen
Davy Dunder Feet
Mrs Freddy Cheesecake
Effie Pull-the-plug
Heilan Merrag
The Bit o' Bud
The Black Japan
Crunch
Fiddy Doddler
Diddy Foddler
Foddy Diddler
Doddy Fiddler!
Jimmy Neep
Sammy Dreep
Captain Skarfie
Ha' Will
Baffin Bay
The Bullet
Coalie Jimmack
The Chicken
Onion
Penguin
Young Pia
Owld Pia
Tiger
Happy Harry

Willie Come Lately
Owld Bilcum
Young Bilcum
Sniff
Clootie
Gobbie
Billy Ballet
Toffee Jim
The Roosh
Brown Owl
Bella Yap
Mother-of-Pearl
Ten-tae-two
Tipenny Dip
Tammy Troot
Tillywup
Bill Squeaks
The Goose
Shoot the Otter
Jock Feet
Blocky Bill
Slavery Dod
The Ship's Cat

And many more!

> *A cheil's amang ye takin notes –*
> *and faith, he'll prent it!*

Robert Burns

'What are you doing these days?'
  'I'm writing a history of Stromness.'
'Stromness has no history.'
'Another slim volume for our bookshelves!'
'I read the papers from end to end, so I don't have time to read your book.'
  'I'd have read your book, but I don't know Stromness.'
'That's why I've written it.'
'My, you're a good salesman!'

*

'A book about Orkney, yes, but I'll not be reading a book about Graemsay.'
  'I wid read yer book if it wis aboot Shapinsay.'
'I suppose you'll sell half-a-dozen.'

*

I greet a fellow pall bearer at the funeral of a fellow historian:
  'Hello, I hear you are coming into print!'
  'Yes, and it will be a real history by a real historian!'

*

'What are you doing with yourself these days?'
'I'm writing my memoirs.'
'That's a piece of self-indulgence!'

Many years ago T S Eliot ended a poem with a line I would have liked to quote in the following End Piece. And the film star Doris Day sang a relevant verse. Both, I am certain, would have been thrilled to be included, but at the risk of eye-watering copyright fees they've been consigned to the dustbin of eternity.

End Piece

This odyssey began in the midst of a world war, and endures in a world pandemic. Over the past eighty years much has changed in Orkney, and much more will change as we confront the complexities of the modern world. As folk used to say: *We maun tak' a stout hert tae a steep brae.*

ORKNEYOLOGY PRESS

Orkneyology Press is aimed at giving voice to stories that deserve to be heard.

The author delights in joining the publishers, Tom and Rhonda Muir, in toasting you, dear reader, for supporting this venture.

Thanks all